EDUCATION HUMANELY APPLIED

Student Behavior and Teacher Performance

Can Be Improved Humanely in Schools

Marie Phillips, Ph.D.

TABLE OF CONTENTS

DEDICATION ii
ACKNOWLEDGMENTS iii
FOREWORD: EDUCATION HUMANELY APPLIED
        Student Behavior Can Be Improved Humanely in Schools.............. 1
        What Happened? Diversity Training Will Help Teachers
        Relate to Every Student... 6
        What Happened? Jenny's Story... 10
        What Happened? Making Time for Student's Needs 11
CHAPTER I: ORIGIN OF THE STUDY The Restructuring Movement
        and the Block Schedule as a Process 15
        What Happened? Migrant Education in a Washington School 26
        What Happened? Early Experience in Frustration in Using
        the Block Schedule... 33
CHAPTER II: REVIEW OF LITERATURE Effects of Changes in the
        Workplace, Effect of Change on All Those Who Experienced
        Change.. 36
        What Happened? Margaret Chapman and Discrimination............ 42
        What Happened? Counselor/Principal Relations by Jenny Rose... 62
        What Happened? Johnny and the YMCA 70
CHAPTER III: RESEARCH METHODOLOGY Qualitative Research and
        Heuristic Inquiry... 75
        What Happened? Teacher Experiences Board Member Angst...... 86
CHAPTER IV: DATA The Role of the Administrator in Facilitating
        Change and the Components of the Change Process.......................93
        What Happened? Coach Carter 100
        What Happened? Boy Code... 110
CHAPTER V: DISCUSSION OF FINDINGS Themes, Stages of Change,
        Organization of the Scheduling Committee and Training 122
        What Happened? Commencement Speech by the Principal........ 141
CHAPTER VI: CONCLUSION 155
APPENDIX 157
        What Happened? Sarah and her 40th Reunion 159
        The Spokesman Review Guest Editorial 161
BIBLIOGRAPHY.. 164
ABOUT THE AUTHOR 179

What Happened?

Throughout this book, the reader will find sections titled: **What Happened?** Each of these scenarios presents a short story or summary of an incident that is based on an actual occurrence, depicting an incident that further demonstrates how education humanely applied—or not—has impacted students, teachers, administrators, parents, school boards, and/or members of the community. Many of these scenarios have been submitted by administrators who wanted to support this book, and wanted to tell stories that they felt needed to be told. Many of them also chose to present their stories anonymously. For all of the scenarios, the names of characters and settings have been changed to protect the innocent and the guilty.

"The Philosophy of the schoolroom in one generation

is the philosophy of the government in the next."

Abraham Lincoln

DEDICATION

THE KETTLE FALLS HIGH SCHOOL TEACHERS

ii

These amazing, dedicated, competent teachers made the commitment to work together, made difficult compromises, and produced the four-period block schedule. It was a privilege to work with them. I also dedicate this book to the Kettle Falls students, parents, staff, community, school board, and Superintendent John Mathis.

Omak High School staff, through their training and support in our initial phases of change, helped us get a positive, informative start.

Shadle Park High School teachers and administrators made me welcome to research with them as they experienced systemic change. I gained a great deal from this excellent experience because I had the opportunity to observe and record their move to the block schedule and compare it to the Kettle Falls High School process.

I also dedicate this book to my wonderful family members who have supported me through the research and the writing process. I am truly blessed!

ACKNOWLEDGMENTS

I thank every student I have ever taught for being in my classes, on my teams, and a part of the learning and teaching results of many experiences we shared. We had some great moments and some conflicting experiences as we learned from each other. All of these students contributed to my learning and made me a better human being. I appreciate all of the teachers, administrators, staff members, and parents who traveled the same journey and gave their support to our students along our way together. I thank everyone involved in publishing and marketing this book for helping me share my goals for greater success for both students and teachers as they work in schools together. No one succeeds in this world of education alone. We need each other. Respecting each other will bring success to us all as we help all of our students succeed. During my professional career, I have come to know many exceptional educators. I have invited many of them to write "What Happened?" sections of this book. I appreciate them for sharing unique stories about their experiences, and I respect those among this group who wish to remain anonymous. My doctoral experience at Gonzaga University opened this opportunity to research using time differently and the impact it had on educators and students. I thank Reverend Patrick Ford, Dr. Shann Ferch, and Dr. Nancy Isaacson for their guidance through the research process.

FOREWORD: EDUCATION HUMANELY APPLIED

Student Behavior Can Be Improved Humanely in Schools

By Marie Phillips, Ph.D.

While schools are planning to provide a healthy school experience, in-school or online, full-time or part-time, I encourage everyone involved in schools to take a strong look at the long-practiced system of assigning punishment for various infractions, which are listed in The Student Handbook for many of the approximately 98,000 public schools in the USA *(usually online: look up the school name. When on that site, input "Student Handbook" and find the rules and consequences for behavior infractions).* I have been both teacher and administrator in Washington State schools and four other states, and as I look back over my years as an educator, I see clearly now what I deeply wish I would have seen throughout my earlier teaching and administration career. Too often, we lose students from school by trying to punish them into cooperating instead of guiding them more creatively toward success; beginning in pre-school and continuing through every grade, we have the privilege of guiding them. Public school discipline systems are patterned in the military. Make a soldier strong—hold him/her accountable through punishment. One error could cost the loss of many lives. Let's be clear: students are not soldiers. Yes, students need accountability, but no, accountability does not have to be taught through negative consequences. This is a national issue, not just in Washington State. It is a practice that targets minorities and boys most and just about every student at some point in his or her Pre-K-12 experience.

Most student handbooks list consequences when a student is tardy. Punishments include detentions, and if tardies continue, then suspensions are often the next level, separating tardy students from school for a full day at a time. Another disciplinary section involves unexcused absences with consequences that include in-school and out-of-school suspensions, where students are often unable to make up work—and may eventually face expulsion. Students coming back to school following a suspension are behind academically in every class because they missed instruction. These students are often left to survive on their own. If they cannot catch up successfully, they may fail classes. In cases where students are given assignments to complete while serving suspensions, they may not know how to do the assigned work since they missed class instruction; as a result, they may not be able to complete it. Students returning to class after disciplinary action may feel embarrassed, unwelcome, angry, unable to understand the class work, bullied by other students—and even shamed by some teachers, as well as other students. We need a behavior system based on keeping students in school, not having them work their way toward expulsion, and facing the difficulties that may follow. Punitive separation from school could negatively affect the rest of their lives.

More boys than girls receive major consequences for several reasons—lack of maturity, more aggressiveness, lack of awareness of how their behavior influences others. Girls also have these issues, but they may tend to hold back more and be more hesitant to lead with distractive behaviors. Once students get known for missing school or settling for failure, they may not see a way through their situations. And worse, for many of these students, discrimination rears up to crush them as well. Students of color receive many more disciplinary suspensions and expulsions than white students.

According to www.discriminology.org., 70% of law enforcement referrals from schools are minority students: Black, Latino, American Indian. Over 68% of male prisoners in federal prison do not have high school diplomas. Homelessness, unemployment, drug abuse, mental illness, crime, and prison are stronger possibilities for non-graduates. We CAN figure this out. As a high school principal, I assigned a student to "On Task," a less negative word for "in-school suspension." While the student was "On Task" in school, teachers provided the work the student had missed during truancy, as well as class work being missed while "On Task." During the time "On Task," teachers made at least two visits to the student during the school day to encourage the student and to make sure the student knew how to do the work. The counselor met at least twice with the student to see what other issues may be impeding success. I also met with the student for further support, brought him or her lunch, and gave positive feedback as appropriate. When the student came to school the next day, his or her class work was up to date, and the staff were supportive. For most students, one day like this was a major cure for truancy. So much positive attention can deter negative behavior, and when a student is totally prepared for the school day, he or she is unafraid of teacher pressures or feeling lost in the lesson.

Our "On Task" was successful by teachers' standards mainly because, when word got out about the attention students received, many potential offenders decided they didn't want to get into trouble. The program was successful by students' standards because grades improved, attendance improved, and there were very few second-time-around offenders. Teachers made the best of their individual time with students and indicated that they were able to establish positive connections with students who had previously been unwilling to participate in the class or complete their assignments

Sometimes students face horrendous issues at home that cause them to be late or absent. Students arrive at school with their lives in their heads. When was their last meal? What are their home lives like? Do they even have a home? Do they have a disability that is not being treated—maybe even not noticed or diagnosed? Are they holding down jobs to feed their families? Students from wealthy homes may also be deprived of love, attention, appropriate nourishment, or other needs for a positive living experience. Any student may be the target of some sort of abuse—physical, sexual, neglect, loneliness, bullying, and other mental and physical hardships. Continuing to punish students for behaviors resulting from reasons they cannot control is frustrating for all concerned and certainly not productive in any positive way.

Students come to school with all their issues, and we need to keep them attending and successful, not shut them out. Some students take a stand to reject help. Some students are amazingly hard to work with or have undiagnosed disabilities, but we cannot give up on them. Every student shapes our nation's future. School personnel must meet students where they are and guide them toward making choices that enrich their future. Helping them get the services they may need may require parent conferences, special education referrals, counseling referrals, and/or medical attention through their families or through public health services. The Community School, a public high school in Spokane, Washington, has a principal and staff who focus on students succeeding. Serious disciplinary issues usually begin with a parent-student-principal conference to find a new path to success. When students have conflicts with one another, the principal brings them together to find ways these students can resolve issues between them instead of letting anger bring future unrest. If this school can take the fear of punishment out of school, other schools with a punishment focus can redirect, and do this, too. I know that there are many schools that are meeting this challenge with success.

Too many schools are stuck in the past and keep doing what has always been done: make a mistake—get punished. This format may have been a military training influence. The usual punishment system is failing too many students. According to www.datacenter.kidscount.org, in the 2015-2016 school year, 3.4 million children ages 6-17 repeated at least one grade since starting kindergarten.

Students who repeat grades are likely to perform poorly in school, experience emotional and behavioral consequences, and drop out of school. According to www.huffpost.com, in 2019, 3.45 million students were suspended from school, and 130,000 students were expelled. Counselors, administrators, teachers, and staff need to focus their attention on students' well-being and look for ways to keep students in school, help them keep up with their peers, and not seek out rule infractions to punish them out of class attendance. Students deserve better than isolation and rejection when they make mistakes.

The feedback I have heard from educators who can't imagine themselves having to give up all the rules includes the following: "We've always done it this way," or "You have to punish them, or they'll just do it again," or "It's too much effort to change every school." One middle school teacher told me, "Some students just don't belong in school. They aren't safe, they don't even try to succeed, and they take up time I should be spending on students who do try to be successful."

For some middle school and high school teachers who have reached this level of frustration with school, I have to wonder when their students first started their path to failure and what situations occurred that made these students find themselves out of touch or angry with the school. Beginning the positive, welcoming atmosphere in school, including pre-school and all grades throughout the system, requires constant nurturing and must be continuously applied throughout the years for each student. I say to this middle school teacher—"Do not give up on this student. If you can't help him or her, let's find someone who can." Teachers can often support and advise one another to find ways to keep a student in school without hardship to other students. Continuing to punish students for behaviors resulting from reasons they cannot control is frustrating for all concerned and certainly not productive in any positive way.

Teachers also arrive at school with their personal and professional lives guiding their school interactions with colleagues, other employees, and students they easily relate to, as well as students they would prefer not to teach some days. If a high school English teacher has thirty-five students per class, six classes per day, and no assistance from an aide, that teacher may not feel ready to be all things to all of her or his students all day long. Teachers can be set in their ways, caught up in the rules game, and can be ready to hand out detentions for all sorts of infractions. So much to do, so little time. "How do I accomplish the impossible?" the frustrated teachers say to no one in particular because they do not believe anyone is listening. Unfortunately, not enough people are listening.

Now let's bring frustrated students to classes with frustrated teachers and see just how successful all of them feel at the end of any school day. Many students get discouraged and drop out. Many teachers get discouraged and change careers. We need to lower the dropout rate for both students and teachers.

The supervisor of teachers, often the principal, may approach her or his evaluation of the classroom teachers' role as the time to observe teachers and look for any way to help them become better teachers. Sometimes administrators search for problems, errors, and ways to make teachers and staff members improve. Often this goal to find problems becomes so strong that all the teacher or staff member gets is negative feedback, orally and in writing—a list of errors, mistakes, "what you should do," and a timeline to reach perfection. The evaluator needs to find something positive before beginning the evaluation process. "Something positive" may have occurred a few weeks prior to the evaluation—or on the same day. Leaving out the positive performance, however hard to find, in my opinion, is teacher abuse and a sign that the principal is not visiting classes and interacting enough with teachers. If the positive is as little as "Hey, when you showed up today and held the door for those students, they were smiling at you! Nice!" or "That bulletin board shows creativity as it clearly targeted your science unit!" or "I appreciated your positive comment in the staff meeting—it shows you really understand that issue."

If we truly want to guide students toward an America where homelessness, overcrowded prisons, unemployment, and other social issues become drastically reduced, we have to treat all of our students with respect—every day. To make that happen, we need to treat our educators with respect—every day. I believe we can do that if we will just look at what we are doing and find ways to lift us all out of the habit of punishing students—and teachers. Let's seek success through respect and kindness. Change will not be easy, but what we are doing now isn't easy, either—and it isn't providing enough positive results for students or teachers. We can do this together. I have lists of alternatives to punishment for students for a variety of infractions that I will share in the appendix. I also have noted specific examples of incidents in "What Happened?" inserts throughout the book to show "What worked" (or did not work) and alternative possibilities that could have worked with a different approach. These incidents are real, although names have been changed to protect the innocent—and the guilty.

For those who say that this is too hard, impossible, and too much to ask, I want to point out that women getting the right to vote was hard. Stopping slavery was hard. Monumental changes are hard but absolutely necessary and well worth our effort to improve the way we want our future to look. Students are our future. Teachers are their guides to success. *Education Humanely Applied* will potentially provide a brighter future for our nation.

<u>whwhwhwhwhwhwhwhwhwhwhwhwhwhwhwhwhwhwhwhwhwhwhwh</u>

What Happened?

Diversity Training Will Help Teachers Relate to Every Student

Teachers and administrators know that they need to work with every child or young adult in their classrooms. Unfortunately, for some students, the teacher or administrator "knowing" doesn't translate to the teacher or administrator "doing" the job by respecting each student as an individual with a multitude of diverse issues. In some cases, there is an absence of "knowing" or "doing" on the part of educators.

Goals in offering diversity training are designed to help educators develop a more in-depth understanding of "diversity" and how they can find ways to learn how to show respect and kindness to every student, every day, in the many usual and unusual situations they face, and their students face, every day.

Usual: race, ethnicity, gender, religion, physical handicap.
Unusual: non-visual race, unnamed religion, political influence, undiagnosed handicap, the target of physical and/or emotional abuse at home/school, employment, caring for an ill family member(s), caring for babies or younger children, homeless, on probation, work required of the family (farming, mechanics, retail, custodial), pregnant, LGBTQ, gang member, married, and so many other individual hardships and rewards.

- Each day brings its own set of circumstances, ready to influence behaviors.
- Every item above can also apply to every teacher and administrator.

What accommodations can employees and professionals provide their students in these usual and unusual situations? School districts need to take appropriate care of teachers and administrators so they may provide their students with the best humane education for students.

Every student has the potential to share with the class his or her ideas, strengths, and talents. Diversity is the exploration and the incorporation of every student's contributions to enrich the learning opportunities for the class. Teachers create an atmosphere of respect for diversity in classes. Administrators open the student body to that diversity.

Educators make that happen when they:

- View each student as an individual capable of success.
- Open our eyes, hearts, and minds to the potential of every student.
- When we truthfully say, "It's NOT ABOUT ME."
- Stop saying, "MY WAY, OR THE HIGHWAY."
- Plan lessons with every student's success as the outcome.
- Stop assigning students embarrassing, isolating consequences.
- Include every student's participation, ideas, creativity, and interests.

Educators need to make a genuine effort to get to know their students and their families.

Here are some ways to help make that happen:

- Parent/student conference regarding positive agenda.
- Assignments that invite personal comments—not force exposure.
  e.g., *our favorite activity/sport/food/holiday and 3 reasons why.
- Use oneself as the main character.
- If you had three wishes, what would they be, and what would the results be if these wishes came true for you—for others.
- Tell why you wanted to make these three specific wishes.
  (Do choices show kindness, shyness, positivity, fear, etc.?)
- Have students select career choices or rejections—why? Why not?
- Plan lessons that reflect more than one learning style to accommodate your students' various learning styles—visual, auditory, tactile, etc.
- Make an appropriate interaction with every student twice a week or more. Use a seating chart inconspicuously to check off successes and contacts. It is very hard to remember every contact. Leave no one out.
- Make a point to find out the disabilities of students. Communicate appropriately with these students based on their individual needs, and

do not force them to be like every other student if they cannot do so. Students with autism have very different issues, so one method for one will probably not be recommended for every student with autism.
- Be aware that some of your students may have disabilities that have not been diagnosed. Tread lightly, investigate before acting, and never use humiliating or demeaning means to get students to respond as you require.

Teachers and administrators have many ideas, operating methods, and techniques they may have used for years. Taking time to reevaluate these ideas, habits, and techniques in the light of how students will benefit from them will help positive communication and rapport with students—each and every student. As we move to a block schedule, we must take a special interest in every student. Change is going to be difficult for many of them. Our future as a nation can benefit from the "Every student, Every day" approach to administration and teaching. For our nation's future, let's reduce unemployment, homelessness, drug addiction, prison populations, and physical and mental abuse—one student at a time, in every class, every day.

whwhwhwhwhwhwhwhwhwhwhwhwhwhwhwhwhwhwhwhwhwhwhwh

Education Humanely Applied

The second goal of this book, *Education Humanely Applied*, is based on my doctoral dissertation as I researched how time influenced teaching and learning. I was fortunate to work as a high school principal with many teachers in the process of changing the traditional school-day schedule for the improvement of teaching and learning for students and teachers. Schedules that provide longer periods of time, such as three or four periods of 90 to 100-minute classes per day twice per week per class, or schedules that include options for both on-site and online or distance learning, provide more options for students. As a result of this study, I truly believe that the best schedule for any school is the one developed through the participation of all concerned: the school board, administrators, teachers, support staff, students, parents, and community. The school that reflects the ideas of all stakeholders has the best chance of succeeding. Once this is developed, change may occur as needed. The primary goal of this planning is to provide the best educational opportunity for every student. Every student. Not just clean, cooperative students, not just white students, not just smart students, not just typical students—every student. Every color, religion, nationality, mental and physical abilities, and culture. Every day.

If we can accomplish getting children and young adults to earn a high school diploma, we will have given them that first key to employment: being more qualified to get a job. A diploma is a basic, consistent requirement for most jobs. Not having a diploma may lead to homelessness, unemployment, mental health issues, drug abuse, crime, overcrowded prisons, and much more. If we can keep our students in school and guide them toward getting their diplomas, we not only improve students' lives but also raise the quality of life in our nation. If we do not make this change, if we continually punish students by throwing them out or embarrassing them through demeaning consequences, not only do they lose—our whole nation loses.

The cost of upgrading our schools, so they provide a more humane education is not so much about money. It's more about being creative, willing to give up previous ways of operating the punishment systems and developing new respectful ways to modify behaviors and attitudes. It will cost us time to rethink our system. The loss of assigning a punishment and moving on must be replaced with more creative, caring, and positive ways to change behavior. When we accomplish this, we will save funding by reducing homelessness, prison populations, unemployment, and other harms associated with dropping out of school or poorly educating students. Our nation will come out having a much more stable society and better-educated citizens. By learning humane ways to lift our students toward positive behaviors, our nation will experience the success of our students, teachers, and administrators. We cannot continue to follow the status quo by ignoring our responsibility to provide every student with humane education.

I hope schools will develop humane methods of applying consequences that demonstrate kindness and respect toward students and teachers. Imagine how providing humane education can enrich our whole society and produce confident students ready for advanced education, training, and/or employment when they graduate from school. Now imagine continuing to use the military model we presently use: break a rule, get punished, get thrown out of school. When I imagine where many of our young people will end up if we don't stop punishing them, I simply have to keep working to convince others of the imperative need to stop what we are doing and support providing a humane solution.

What Happened?

Jenny's Story

"Jenny" was smoking pot on campus. A staff member brought her to the office, pot in hand. There was no doubt that Jenny had broken a school rule and a state law. Consequences included a principal interview with Jenny, a parent meeting, a police call, and an arrest. The principal assigned suspension until drug rehab and legal consequences were met in an acceptable manner or permanent expulsion if the student did not follow through as the rules required.

What could have happened? Principal conference: The principal COULD say, "Jenny, I am disappointed in you. We can't have your bad example around other students. What were you thinking? I'm really disappointed in you. You are out of here, and I don't want to see you anywhere near this campus again. You really let us down."

What did happen? The principal DID say, "Jenny, the police will be here soon. I can see that you are frightened, and we both wish you had made a better choice here. You have two important choices coming up—cooperating with police and fulfilling the drug rehabilitation program. I encourage you to do what is required. Do what you need to do to get back here. It won't be easy. I know you will get through this. You are stronger than you think, and I believe in you. I want you back in school, Jenny—don't doubt that. Here is my card. Call me if you need to talk." *The principal was sincere in her encouragement.* Jenny fulfilled rehab requirements, returned to school and graduated with her class. She graduated from college and became a nurse.

Jenny could have dropped out of school for good, become dependent on drugs, and/or joined the homeless, unemployed population, or the pipeline to prison due to drug dependency and the absence of support. Society could have been denied one competent nurse whose career could have included saving many lives and treating many wounds.

Part of the learning process, unfortunately, is making mistakes. As teachers and administrators, we can lift students out of their errors by counseling them, helping them through these difficult times, and respecting them while they learn to take responsibility for their actions. Expelling them or encouraging them to leave school by shaming them is simply turning our backs on them and it is not in their best interest or society's best interest in the long run. Can we save them all? Maybe. When we stop punishing and start humanely caring for them as early as pre-school, they will have a much better chance for success.

whwhwhwhwhwhwhwhwhwhwhwhwhwhwhwhwhwhwhwhwhwhwhwh

whwhwhwhwhwhwhwhwhwhwhwhwhwhwhwhwhwhwhwhwhwhwhwh

What Happened?

Making Time for Student's Needs

Why do Autistic Kids Make Easy Targets for School Bullying?

Bullying can lead to depression, low grades, behavioral problems, and even physical illness because of the stress it causes — and kids with autism may be suffering the brunt of the harm.

A new study finds that children with autism spectrum disorder are bullied nearly five times as often as their typically developing peers. Parents of autistic kids think the rate is even higher than that. In the study, about 46% of autistic children in middle and high school told their parents they were victimized at school within the previous year compared with just over 10% of children in the general population. Author Paul Sterzing (2017) of Washington University in St. Louis told the New York Times that the "rate of bullying and victimization among these adolescents is alarmingly high." He called it a "profound public health problem."

Many people with autism have trouble recognizing social cues, which makes them awkward around others. They also often engage in repetitive behaviors and tend to be hypersensitive to environmental stimuli, all of which makes students with the disorder ripe targets for bullies who hone in on differences and enjoy aggravating their victims. About a third of autism cases are severely disabled. Those affected may suffer from low IQ and be unable to talk. But most autistic people have average or high intelligence and many can function well if their social and sensory issues are appropriately addressed. That may help explain why the highest functioning children in the current study were at the greatest risk of being bullied. While their social awkwardness was more obvious because they actually interacted more with mainstream peers, this made their actual disability less visible, likely making their condition harder for their peers to understand.

Children with autism who could speak well, for example, were three times more likely to be bullied than those whose conversational ability was limited or absent. Further, those who were mainly educated in mainstream classrooms were almost three times more likely to be bullied than those who spent most of their time in special education. Bullying can take the form of teasing, exclusion, humiliation or physical assault, and can lead to depression and other mental health problems, poor grades and physical illness in victims because of the severe stress it causes.

Parents of autistic children think that the true rates of victimization are far higher than what the study found, and that the rates of perpetrating bullying are lower, precisely because autism disorders are characterized by an inability to read subtle social cues and by difficulty with communication. In order to report being bullied, students need to understand when they are being targeted. In contrast, students also need to understand and effectively deploy harassing social information in order to be a bully. Understanding this type of social information is something that autistic children generally cannot do. Impaired language skills and inability to read social cues also mean that many autistic children are bullied without ever realizing it or being able to report it. Riley-Hall recalled an incident involving her daughter in elementary school. "Little boys were getting her to say dirty words and laughing at her. She thought this was a good thing and that they were being friendly, but they were really making fun of her," she said, describing how another girl, who knew it was wrong, told the teacher. But until the classmate reported it, Riley-Hall had no idea that her daughter was being bullied—nor did her daughter. NOTE: The article by Maia Szalavitz may be found at the address by the author's name: MaiaSzalavitz@maiasz.com

The article also notes that teachers are also often unaware that bullying is occurring. Students who bully often are quite good at finding times and places to carry out their bullying when no staff members are present. Teachers and staff at times do nothing to correct bullying, perhaps thinking that students can work it out on their own. This, of course, makes it worse for the autistic student who gets bullied, who doesn't have the skills to deal with it, and who sees no one willing to help him—even staff members whom he or she sees actually witnessing the abuse. Fear of reprisal also keeps students from reporting. Students are afraid that a parent will say something: "It'll get worse, Mom. Please don't tell." Parents feel like they take a risk in telling school staff, and when they do tell, they fear the problem may not be resolved—and may escalate. Yet nothing can be corrected by failing to report.

whwhwhwhwhwhwhwhwhwhwhwhwhwhwhwhwhwhwhwhwhwhwhwh

Make Time to Meet Student and Teacher Needs for Optimal Learning Opportunities

This qualitative study with elements of heuristic inquiry examines the professional and personal impact of change on ten teachers and two administrators in Shadle Park High School in Spokane, Washington. The change involved moving from a traditional schedule to an AB block schedule. Interviews with two administrators and dialogues with ten teachers, along with several on-site visitations, provided the data for this study. The heuristic element developed due to the author's participation in a four-year period of research, planning, and implementation of a block schedule while serving as principal at Kettle Falls High School in Kettle Falls, Washington. Experiences shared by Shadle Park High School teachers and administrators are compared and contrasted with the author's experiences in Kettle Falls High School.

Research questions guiding the study included: Is there meaningful change for teachers in presenting lessons in longer time frames? Are there emotional changes for participants, and if so, what are those emotional changes? What role do administrators play in the change process? Do professional educators give up anything in moving to a block schedule? The focus of this study was to examine the change process and its effects on teachers and administrators who move from the traditional schedule to the block schedule.

Findings indicated that the change process can be exceptionally difficult for groups and individuals. In order for change to occur, individuals must decide to change and follow through, regardless of their personal and/or professional discomfort or pain. Findings noted that change brings about both physical and emotional reactions, which are based on each individual's receptiveness to the change process. Physical changes included reformatting class exercises and teaching delivery systems. Emotional changes included frustration, anger, fear, confusion, and feelings of success or failure. Advance preparation, ongoing training, scheduling time for teachers to learn, open communication among administrators and teachers, as well as teachers sharing among themselves, as they all explore the challenges they experience will ease reactions to problems incurred as a result of the change process. Recommendations for future research in this area include quantitative studies of teachers' specific reactions to change and qualitative studies of specific schools, faculties, and portions of faculties that are experiencing change.

CHAPTER I: ORIGIN OF THE STUDY

The Restructuring Movement and the Block Schedule as a Process

Beginning in 1992, while serving as high school principal of Kettle Falls High School in Kettle Falls, Washington, I had the opportunity to work with a teaching staff that wanted to improve the curriculum as well as other aspects of the school. These teachers did not have a specific plan to make the changes they felt were necessary. The teachers as a group wanted to research better ways to organize time for themselves and their students, and they wanted their students to be more successful on standardized tests as well as in their classrooms. The Washington State Legislature passed Senate Bill 2953 in 1991, creating the Commission on Student Learning, which organized a statewide approach to public school reform. Information from the Office of Public Instruction also promoted interest among Kettle Falls High School teachers in their efforts to improve their system.

At the time, Omak High School in Omak, Washington, had been experimenting with block scheduling. One of the Kettle Falls teachers brought to a staff meeting a pamphlet (Neimeyer, 1992) that had been put together by the Omak teaching staff. As a result of staff interest in the contents of that pamphlet, our staff sent a team of six staff members, including me, to visit Omak High School. We participated in a block schedule presentation that Omak faculty members had organized for several groups from schools in Washington.

Our team included a vocational teacher, a math teacher, a special education teacher, a social studies teacher, an English teacher, and me, the principal of the high school, representing the administration. We participated in the overview of the change process. Each of us also had time to visit with other professionals in our specific teaching and administration areas. As a result of our visit to Omak, we returned to Kettle Falls High School and shared what we had learned with our colleagues. Our information sharing prompted other teachers to want to make visitations. The second team included six teachers, a board member, three students, and two parents. Several staff members and I also reviewed current educational literature and studies of other secondary school reforms. (Carroll,

Glasser, Goodlad, and Singh were among the authors whose works we studied in regard to restructuring).

Because of our research, visitations, and the restructuring committee's efforts in working with our community, students, parents, and school board, Kettle Falls High School moved to a four-period block schedule in 1993. At the present time (2022), Kettle Falls is still operating under a similar form of block scheduling. In adopting this schedule, the change the participants experienced was greater than any of us had anticipated. The act of changing to a schedule that lengthened each period from 50 minutes to 90 minutes affected far more than the bell schedule.

As a result of experiencing the change in the block schedule in Kettle Falls, when I entered the doctoral program at Gonzaga University in Spokane, Washington, I chose to study at a high school in its first year of implementing a block schedule as my dissertation program. Questions I hoped to answer included: Is there a meaningful change for teachers in presenting lessons in this longer time frame? Are there emotional changes for the participants, and if so, what are these emotional changes? What role do administrators play in this change process? Do professional educators give up anything in moving to a block schedule? The focus of this study is to examine the change process and its effects on teachers who move from the traditional schedule to the block schedule.

Purpose of the Study

This qualitative inquiry examined the process of a change from a traditional schedule to a block schedule as it touched the lives of ten teachers and two administrators in one urban school, Shadle Park High School in Spokane, Washington, with approximately 1,500 students. I chose a qualitative study because of my professional and personal experience as an administrator and participant in a similar change process at Kettle Falls High School. By observing the change process at Shadle Park High School, I hope to more fully comprehend my own past experiences in moving to a block schedule. By examining the process as other educators are experiencing it, I hoped to gain a deeper understanding of how change affects these educators. The purpose of the study was to examine how change affected the teachers as professional educators, to examine how teachers personally internalized the expectations of change, and to share the impact of this change on the teachers and administrators in this study with others considering similar changes.

The results of change for one school district as it moved from the traditional schedule to the block schedule may offer other educators or persons involved in schedule changes in other schools some insight into their own concerns related to change. This study of one city high school in its first year of a block schedule offers other educators one view of the change process through members of one teaching staff and two administrators. Their experiences may provide a combination of similar and contrasting data for other educators involved in developing and implementing various types of block schedules. The process of change that the teachers experienced may serve as a catalyst for discussion among others who have attempted change, who are considering change of any kind, or who find change being thrust upon them.

Because I approached this qualitative research with elements of heuristic inquiry, I must be mindful of researcher bias. As I interviewed two administrators and had dialogues with ten teachers, I needed to let them speak for themselves. I will discuss researcher bias more fully when I share methodology information in Chapter 3.

Definition of Terms

- The definition of the following terms may provide an understanding of their use in the context of this research:
- *Change:* the process of learning or relearning to perform in a new or different way; to think in a new or different way; to apply new or different materials and/or techniques (Fullan and Hargreaves).
- *Block schedule:* a lengthening of classroom time from the traditional period of 45 to 55 minutes to various lengths of time that may run from 70 minutes to several hours per day. The block of time is developed into a pattern for daily, weekly, monthly, and/or a yearly plan of instructional time (Ballinger, Carroll, Neimeyer, Thomas).
- *Traditional schedule or factory model:* a schedule based on six, seven, or eight periods of time per day. Each period of 45 to 60 minutes per period has from three to five minutes of passing time between classes. Students generally move from class to class, meeting with a different teacher and subject each period (Ballinger, Carroll).
- *Term:* a period of time in which credit for courses is completed (Carroll, Neimeyer).

- ***Semester:*** half of a traditional school year (Neimeyer). *Implementation of* or *implementing change:* putting programs, processes, and/or formats for schedules or other changes into practice for the first time in a particular setting and/or with a group of people who have no previous experience of the change (Fullan).

Background of the Current Restructuring Movement in Public Schools

This section outlines recent historical governmental involvement in analyzing the condition of education, as well as professional educators' views of educational excellence—or lack thereof. The 1983 publication of *A Nation at Risk* is the first of the recent historical publications that influenced the national focus on education. This section concludes with Washington state's current efforts to improve K-12 education.

In 1983, Terrill Bell, the United States Secretary of Education, formed the National Commission on Excellence in Education. The goal of this Commission was to evaluate the quality of American education. The report that resulted from the research and evaluation of this Commission was called *A Nation at Risk: The Imperative for Educational Reform.* (Commission on Excellence in Education, 1983). This report influenced the public's perception of education. Major newspapers, magazines, as well as radio and television media gave this report attention that brought national concern for the quality of this nation's public schools.

Secondary education was described in this report as having a secondary curriculum without a central purpose. Because of the widespread course offerings that have been added to the curriculum, *A Nation at Risk* indicated that secondary schools spend too little time teaching quality material and too much time teaching nonessential, nonacademic information. The Commission's report stated, "Secondary school curricula have been homogenized, diluted, and diffused to the point that they no longer have a central purpose . . . we have a cafeteria-style curriculum in which the appetizers and desserts can easily be mistaken for the main course." (Commission on Excellence in Education, 1983, p. 24).

The Commission's report gave an overview of educational statistics on functional illiteracy in our adult population, comparison scores of United States public school students and scores of students of many other nations of the world, and the academic achievement levels of minority youth since Sputnik was launched in 1957. Public schools, in response to Sputnik, added math and science courses to the public school curriculum in the late 1950s and early 1960s in an effort to compete with the Soviet Union and regain respect in the race for space. The report indicated that average achievement was lower in 1983 than it was when Sputnik was launched; 23 million Americans were illiterate; United States students were scoring significantly lower on basic academic subjects than students of other nations, and as many as 40% of America's minority youth were functionally illiterate (Commission on Excellence in Education, 1983).

The information from this report may have been the impetus for leading educators to study the American public educational system and publish books addressing educational reform. Publications in 1983 and 1984 that targeted public educational problems and expressed the need for reforming or restructuring schools included many works by prominent educators. Three examples of such publications are: Theodore Sizer's _Horace's Compromise: The Dilemma of the American High School_ (1984); John Goodlad's _A Place Called School_ (1984); Seymour Sarason's _Schooling in America: Scapegoat and Salvation_ (1983).

In 1991, George Bush endorsed America 2000, An Educational Strategy, a plan with specific goals to improve the quality of the national system of education. Reynolds and Parker (1992) noted that with presidential concern focused on the importance of improving education, states began looking more resolutely at ways to restructure education. The areas of concern included what schools offer and its quality, how teachers deliver information, how students learn, and the time frame in which they learn. Reynolds and Parker pointed out that restructuring became a major focus nationally in public education.

Washington state's restructuring direction has involved many school districts since 1991. The Commission on Student Learning, created through the legislature, set up advisory boards whose membership included teachers, parents, and business leaders (Commission on Student Learning, 1996). These advisory boards wrote benchmarks for the core curriculum areas. Teachers throughout Washington public schools in grades K-12 have implemented these benchmarks into their curriculum. The results may have a major impact on the elementary curriculum and even more impact on secondary schools' curriculum, course offerings, and the structure of courses and schedules. The Washington State Comprehensive Plan for the Improvement of Student Learning, drafted on February 1, 1996, and distributed among Washington schools in December of 1996, is an updated summary of past CSL information and a product authorized by the state legislature. This plan outlined a program for the development of educational policies to improve public education in Washington state (Commission on Student Learning, 1996).

The Washington legislature has provided Student Learning Improvement Grants which have authorized funding for restructuring curriculum to meet these state requirements. The Legislature allocated approximately $75.8 million to Washington schools between 1993 and 1995 and $103.4 million between 1995 and 1997, with indications of continued educational funding forthcoming (Commission on Student Learning, 1996, p. 5). Grant funding targeted teacher training as a prime use of funds. The Commission on Student Learning directed Educational Service Districts to set up workshops, seminars, and conferences for Washington educators.

Many school districts have analyzed their school structure in more than just curriculum guidelines. In revising the curriculum, teachers and administrators have been reviewing how they present information to students. According to Slaven and the National Association of Secondary School Principals, educators are studying students' learning styles and teachers' teaching styles. Schools have been analyzing how they are using the time to meet students' educational needs. Some schools in the review of the nine-month calendar year have questioned the educational benefits of that time frame. Thomas (1973) presented a year-round school program that influenced some schools to consider changing from the agrarian-based nine-month school year. Carroll (1989) introduced a model that provided another use of time-related to individual course selections. Students concentrated on one or two classes at a time through their completion instead of six or seven different classes each day. This model of block scheduling influenced many educators to look at school time differently.

Washington State, in communicating to school districts interested in using time in different ways, has granted variances from the class unit of 150 hours of seat time per credit and has provided that existing requirements may be waived. Schools receiving this waiver present programs that include endorsement by local educators, parents, community members, and the school board. According to Anderson (1996), innovative block schedules occur in approximately 10% of Washington schools. Anderson described four-period block schedules and three-period block schedules, which meet for various numbers of days per year to fulfill credit requirements. As of 2020-21, 51% of Washington schools use some form of block scheduling, and 31% to 50% of our nation's high schools use a form of block scheduling (Chen, 2020). Time has been the key to the restructuring of the schedule. Some schools are analyzing how they have been using time and how they might use it more efficiently to provide optimal learning opportunities for a student. Larger blocks of time improve learning opportunities for students, as well as planned instruction for teachers in presenting lessons and accommodating students' many and varied learning styles.

Making the most productive use of time to improve the educational process appears to have been the motivating force for many of the block scheduling designs. Areas of concern included how to reduce the time required to move from class to class, class start-up time and wrap-up time, and administrative paperwork in maintaining student records. According to Neimeyer (1992), students' safety has consistently been a growing concern. Could a different way of using time improve safety factors for students and teachers? Time has shown that fewer passing times per day made a major difference in the number of behavior violations and incidents of bullying. Both students and teachers had improved attendance, as well as a more positive attitude about school.

School districts, in evaluating block scheduling, have examined their own goals and missions for students and parents, as well as for their communities. The traditional model of seven instructional periods per day for nine months of the year was a way of operating that was seldom questioned. Thomas (1973) pointed out that the fact that schools have functioned that way for over a century seemed to justify the tradition. The three-month summer break was established when agriculture was a leading way of life for most of the people in this country. According to Ballinger (1993), less than 3% of the nation's population in 1993 was involved in agriculture in the traditional manner of the 19th and early 20th centuries. Steven Zahniser (2020) indicated that less than 6% of the GNP involves agriculture. With the potential of a full year of school time to analyze, and the option of designing different time systems for instruction, many school districts have developed innovative plans tailored to their communities and their students, not building the school schedule around the farm schedule.

Block scheduling involves using a period of time larger than the traditional 45- or 50-minute period consistently or in varied patterns in the school schedule. Carroll (1989) set up one- or two-period days of a month or two-month duration for the completion of one or two classes at a time. Kettle Falls High School and Omak High School used a four-period day. Students attended four classes daily for half of the school year and four different classes for the second half of the school year. Each class period was 85 or 90 minutes long. Shadle Park High School in Spokane, Washington, which is the subject of this study, used blocks that were 100 minutes long, three blocks per day, four days per week. On the first day of each week, students attended all six classes; half of the periods met Tuesdays and Thursdays, and the other half met Wednesdays and Fridays. Shadle Park High School still offers a unique schedule (2021) with three classes alternating Mondays and Wednesdays and three different classes on Tuesdays and Thursdays with time set aside in afternoon blocks for individual and group learning opportunities.

The options for blocks of time offer many creative designs in the development of school schedules. A block of time may travel through a week in an otherwise traditional schedule, occurring only once per day. According to Singh (1992), the variety of schedules is wide, creative, and unique to meet individual needs. These examples represent only a fraction of the many programs in place throughout Washington and the nation.

Schools as Organizations in the Change Process

Newmann (1993) indicated that in order for change to be successful, schools, like any other organizations, tend to seek a process to follow that will help ensure that change is really what they need and that the chosen change is the one that will fit the school and community. More specifically, Newmann stated that the change needs to be student-centered as the guiding value for systemic change. Murphy (1991) pointed out that effective change requires a plan. Prior to plan development, the school district that is supportive of change may include in the planning process the participants who will be affected by the change. Teachers may take leadership roles, principals may facilitate change, and superintendents may act as enablers of the process. Authentic power, Webb (1994) explained, which may come from teachers through administrators who support the bottom-up shift in the decisional making, seems to help create an atmosphere for real change to take place. Individual buildings or the district as a whole may see changes. A district-wide philosophy and vision that advocates innovation and change may bring improvement to the district in one building or the entire district.

Joseph Fernandez (1993), Chancellor of New York City Public Schools in 1991 and a leader in school restructuring in New York and Florida, indicated that initiating restructuring involves a shared vision toward change from administrators, teachers, students, and community members. Fernandez supported site-based management in both Dade County in Florida and New York City Public Schools. It takes communication and collaboration with all levels of personnel, evaluation throughout the process, and encouragement to be creative (Hansen and

Liftin, 1991). These basic points, according to Hansen and Liftin, are usually important to establish prior to attempting change. For some districts, getting this level of cooperation may take years. Trying to bring about change in a district or a school that is not interested or not ready to make modifications may be unworkable or unwelcome. I believe districts that make an effort to involve personnel, students, parents, community, and/or other districts when considering major changes often have success in making meaningful change. Fine (1994) noted that the continued use of familiar ways of operating schools and teaching lessons may seem more comfortable to teachers who may not have imagined themselves teaching in any other way but the way they have always taught.

Marris (1974) explained that when change occurs as a result of the involvement of all participants from its inception, the results tend to have positive outcomes. The process of change can be difficult, however, when a school board or an administrator makes a decision that imposes change on others. Marris shared that whether a change is voluntary or a newly assigned task, without any input, "All real change involves loss, anxiety, and struggle" (p. 2). When doing business as usual becomes different, those involved in making the adjustments have both professional and personal concerns. These concerns may be difficult to cope with and may require considerable and unique allowances for some individuals for effective change to take place. Schon (1971) indicated that "passing through the zones of uncertainty equates to the situation of being at sea, of being lost, of confronting more information than you can handle" (p. 12). Ford (1995) contended that "our experiences of change is that change is at the very least a difficult and awkward experience which contains within itself the potential for great qualitative and quantitative growth" (p. 1).

Fullan (1991) asserted that change, with its potential for growth, creates a great deal of unrest and confusion among participants. Understanding this phenomenon can help all of the participants become a cooperating entity, a social system, with common goals and common frustrations. Without that understanding, Fullan (1991) pointed out that frustration can become unbearable. Zaltman and Duncan (1977) defined change as a re-learning by individuals or groups. The re-learning process may vary considerably from person to person and from group to group. The degrees of re-learning required to carry out changes in restructuring fluctuate, depending upon one's receptivity to the change. Fullan pointed out that pain and loss accompany change to varying degrees. Involvement from the beginning of the process may help reduce anxiety and frustration, but even people who are part of the entire process may experience pain, loss, frustration, and confusion throughout the change development and application process.

I believe that teachers are important in any structural change process within education. When the schedule changes, the potential exists to affect every teacher in the system. Meeting a different time frame for the delivery of information may create a need to alter the curriculum, as well as lesson plans, which teachers have used successfully in a familiar schedule. Until I personally participated in the block schedule restructuring process, I did not realize the breadth of the impact across the faculty that block scheduling had in both academic and vocational areas. Some teachers stated that this change reinforced their desire to teach. Other teachers declared that they were glad that their retirement was not far away. I could see that teachers were experiencing a variety of emotional responses as they attempted to cope with changing to the block schedule. Fullan (1991) explained, "Change is needed because many teachers are frustrated, bored, and burnt out. Good change processes that foster sustained professional development over one's career and lead to student benefits may be one of the few sources of revitalization. Other negative emotional responses are an integral part of change, which people experience uniquely and differently.

Students may make a major difference in how schools adjust to change. Fullan (1991) stated, "Educational change, above all, is a people-related phenomenon for each and every individual. Students, even little ones, are people too. Unless they have some meaningful role (to them) in the enterprise, most educational change, indeed most education, will fail" (p. 170). Change that brings students into the process and helps them see their roles as participants, according to Fullan, has a better chance to succeed. When Kettle Falls High School examined schedules, the students met to explore several schedules and discuss which options they would like to investigate. Parents and community members were involved in meetings prior to any decisions on a specific schedule. The results of the students and parents being involved in the planning stages and then in the decision-making process may have contributed to the positive support students and the community members gave when the final schedule was put into place.

Firestone and Rosenblum (1998) researched commitment in regard to teachers and students: "Students respond to the 'respect' shown them by the teacher, the amount of interesting work, and the patience and caring of the teacher in explaining and re-explaining" (p. 11). When students have meaningful involvement in the change process, teachers and principals are demonstrating the respect that Firestone and Rosenblum indicated is important for students. This support may have the potential to help students adjust more easily to change. Principals in particular, have a supportive role for the other participants. I believe that the principal, viewed as the school leader who serves in supportive roles, has a unique opportunity to enable other participants to become involved and move into change with less apprehension.

Berman and McLaughlin (1977) stated that the actions of principals have a positive effect on the success of the rest of the staff, the students, and the community. "Projects having the active support of the principal were most likely to fare well" (p. 124), contended Berman and McLaughlin. Principals may have a pivotal position that could bring all of the participants together as they help keep the mission and goals of the school in focus, as well as the best educational interests of the students. I believe that administrators play an essential role, perhaps the key role, in the success of change efforts that affect students, teachers, and community members.

Research on Educational Change as a Process

A large quantity of research on change is available for study, and when a school district decides to change its system in some way, consulting research may be an important step in moving toward change. Bethany (1991), Fullan (1991), Lieberman (1986), and Miller (1990) indicated that taking advantage of research in the area of change a school is considering can provide valuable information for participants and can assist in determining the direction the district may want to explore. For change to take hold and be successful, Hargreaves (1994) indicated that the people functioning within the school actually make the change a reality. Hargreaves stated, "Political and administrative devices for bringing educational change usually ignore, misunderstand, or override teachers' own desires for change. Such devices commonly rely on principles of compulsion, constraint, and contrivance to get teachers to change" (p. 11).

Research on the process of change has provided many ideas, studies of changes in schools, surveys of reactions to changes, and how the process worked or did not work in various ways. Whether change is welcomed or whether it is a directive assigned to those who make the change, teachers, administrators, and students are the main agents of change in schools. The results of change may depend upon the willingness and the abilities of these change agents to create an acceptable environment that has incorporated the targeted change. Both Sarason (1990) and Hargreaves (1994) have expressed concern about teachers' capacity and desire for change. Teachers who try to fulfill the change while at the same time have classrooms filled with students who need to be taught may reach high frustration levels. If teachers are not receptive to the change, I believe they may outwardly do what they must. When their classroom doors are shut, the expected changes simply may not be done well—or perhaps not done at all. The educational change appears to be a complex, multifaceted experience.

whwhwhwhwhwhwhwhwhwhwhwhwhwhwhwhwhwhwhwhwhwhwhwhwh

What Happened?

Migrant Education in a Washington School

A Washington State Principal's Reflection upon Migrant Education in his School District

The parents had worked hard, sold or gave away their belongings, and planned every single item they placed into family backpacks in preparation for their journey to freedom. Two parents, two children. Nothing extra. As their transport vehicle traveled along very bumpy roads, they sensed that their sixteen-hour journey was coming to an end. The truck stopped, all of the people were rushed off the truck, and then they were told to wade across the river. They heard gunshots in the distance several times and moved as fast as they could into the dark water. Armed men told them to walk or run with the sun on their right in the morning and on their left at night. Someone would meet them in a few days in the desert.

Six months later, the family was living in a desert tent encampment. The parents had hoped their two children would finally get the opportunity to go to school. No one in the family spoke English, but still—they could learn in school, right? They were moved to a city and into group housing. They finally had a chance to enroll their children in school. That was what schools did—educate! Change lives! They tried to enroll their children several times in several schools, only to be put on waiting lists or told that there was no space for them and to try somewhere else.

When one of their children was finally accepted at a school, their mother was excited and brought her to school early and waited for two hours for the mother and daughter interviews. Maria, the eight-year-old, was given a test. The test provider told her to fill in the answers and leave the completed test at the office. The test was in English. Maria's mother looked at the test Maria was holding, then she took it to the office and explained that Maria doesn't read or even understand English.

"Do you have a way for Maria to take the test by telling someone the answers? She wants so much to learn and to be in school." Mom was kind, patient, and hopeful, holding back tears. The intake process took several months before Maria began attending school. She was the only non-English speaker in her class. Unfortunately, she felt isolated in a class full of students who didn't understand her, nor did they try to understand her, and yes, they bullied her both verbally and physically, isolated her, and often made her cry.

Maria's teacher did not speak any other languages and gave Maria pictures to color, comic books to "read," plain paper and crayons to draw her own pictures, and left her to sit by herself in the classroom, even during recess periods.

What happened? Maria's parents were feeling many emotions: fear was always with them in this new country. They gave up everything they had because they believed they would find a new life of freedom and opportunity. They sought help for their children through their church. Fortunately, they found someone who not only helped them, but also found a school where both of their children could attend and where there would be designated classes for immigrants, both children and adults. All four family members attended. Mom found a part-time job cleaning homes, and Dad found work in construction. A schedule was set up for Mom and the two children to attend school in the morning and early afternoon; Dad attended adult class in the evenings.

What could have happened? As with many migrant individuals and families, staying in their country of origin could have cost them their lives. They could have continued in poverty, uneducated and unemployed. Many people do not know how or where to ask for help, and when they do ask, they get turned away or are not actually heard and are not helped. Many teachers feel lost, angry, or disrespected when they are assigned tasks they do not know how—or want—to do.

How does this relate to this book? In many schools, migrant programs do not exist. Many staff members do not know how to help these students, and a significant number of the teachers and staff do not want to help them. They find ways to ignore migrant students, give them busy work, and justify their unprofessional actions by telling themselves that they already work too hard and cannot take on this "requirement" with so many other students to teach.

We must correct this. Statistically, when migrant children are welcomed into schools, they succeed and even outperform many typical students. Also, statistically, many migrant students who are not welcomed, who are isolated, rejected, or ignored, do not succeed. When given leadership roles in this area, some teachers have developed opportunities for these children, recommended staff development, and found ways to assist one another to make education work for their migrant students. Some teachers refused to cooperate. A few teachers transferred to other schools, resigned, retired, or simply pretended they were teaching these children when, in fact, these teachers were abandoning them in plain sight. This is not "humanely applied education."

We are the land of the free and the home of the brave. These people migrated to America, like so many of our ancestors, to make a new, safe life. Our nation counts on immigration to provide labor for many jobs that are drastically unfilled. We really do need them as much as they need us. We need to provide in-service to teachers who are not serving these students so the teachers know what to teach and how to teach them. Teachers who are successful in teaching these children need to have leadership roles in developing and leading teacher training programs. Change is hard, for sure. But the results of teaching all our people—that includes immigrants—equals creating an educated population. We can do this! We must do this. This is a success story, just waiting for all of us to make it happen.

whwhwhwhwhwhwhwhwhwhwhwhwhwhwhwhwhwhwhwhwhwhwhwhwhwhwhwh

Research on the Block Schedule as a Change Process

Forms of block scheduling have been attempted to help reduce the high school dropout rate. Bottoms and Presson (1991) have indicated that traditional schedules often do not meet the unique needs of the student in danger of dropping out of school or of former students who have already dropped out. Unique programs that offer alternatives, which include taking one course at a time for a shorter portion of the school year, have motivated students to complete courses who had previously demonstrated little interest in school. Former students, in some cases, have returned to complete graduation requirements due to alternative schooling. Bottoms and Presson (1991) have encouraging information on helping to keep students in school, and they have included information on nontraditional types of schedules.

Blank and Scaglione (1992) indicated that block scheduling could contribute to the improvement and integration of academic and vocational programs for students. By using time differently from the short, traditional periods for courses, students in vocational classes may participate more easily in the workplace without sacrificing academic learning in the process. Bringing curricula of the vocational and academic areas into one block with team teachers from both areas has the potential of providing students with opportunities a traditional program may not offer. Carroll (1989) noted that blocks of learning time bring changes in teacher delivery systems while acknowledging that students have different learning styles that may more readily be accommodated in a larger block of time. Blank and Scaglione (1992), Bottoms and Presson (1991), and Carroll (1989) pointed out some potential benefits of block scheduling. A scheduling report from Omak High School is based on one year of using a four-period day schedule. Neimeyer (1992), principal of Omak High School, reported the following:

- Teachers and students have more opportunities for quality time.
- Teachers meet with half the usual number of students per semester.
- Teachers and office personnel spend less time on record keeping.
- Teachers begin and end classes less often—a more productive use of time.
- Stress seems to be reduced for everyone with fewer classes per day.
- Teachers are diversifying their delivery systems. (pp.6-8)

Such potential benefits of block scheduling appear noteworthy; however, the real success of any change may lie in the willingness of those people who carry out the change daily—those who interact with one another to make the change happen. Will teachers continue with the plan to change their teaching delivery systems which some of them have practiced for many years? Hargreaves (1994) asked some questions that address this issue:

- How will teachers actually respond to these changes?
- How *do* teachers change—at this moment or any other?

- What makes teachers change in the face of change, and what makes them dig in their heels and resist?

Questions such as these concern what is commonly referred to as the change process: the practices and procedures, the rules and relationships, the sociological and psychological mechanism that shape the destiny of any change, whatever its content, and which lead it to prosper or falter (p. 10).

Patterson (1997 described a school in the process of moving to a block schedule. This school's scheduling committee, after 90 days of study, was ready to make the recommendation that the school adopt the block schedule. Patterson stated:

The faculty members who were not part of the excitement of developing the block schedule concept asked questions such as:

- What's wrong with what we are doing now?
- How is this going to affect my department and me? How is this going to affect my lessons and activities?
- How can I possibly manage everything else the school demands from my time right now? (p. 11)

Patterson noted that when it comes to change, people tend to think of themselves first. According to Patterson:

It is human nature for people to think of themselves, and acknowledging that does not cast a dark shadow on the nature of people. Acting first out of self-interest does not mean people are selfish or disloyal to the organization. It reflects people's need to conserve their scarce energy points. People can't afford to automatically rally around every change initiative anyone in the organization dreams up. To maintain any sense of resilience in the face of change, individuals must spend their energy on initiatives that have a payoff for them. (p. 10).

Researching the process of developing block schedules, as well as numerous forms of block schedules, may promote agents of change to examine the roles of participants from a personal position. This examination of the research may assist participants in understanding what they will actually experience, and it may prepare them more fully for the difficulties that may occur.

<h1 style="text-align:center">Significance of the Study</h1>

Washington has made extensive progress in bringing schools throughout the state to internalize the established goals of the Commission on Student Learning. The State Department of Education has encouraged schools to restructure in an effort to facilitate changes in curriculum, delivery of information and to provide a more community-based school system for each community in the state. The state has provided many school districts with waivers at each school's request for variances in schedules, seat time requirements per credit toward graduation, and the length of the school day. As an administrator involved in applying for and receiving waivers for the Kettle Falls School District, I have followed the state process on three occasions in applying for a variance due to the four-period block schedule. I have appreciated the state's waiver process because by granting schools waivers, the state appears to encourage change through school restructuring.

Articles on how to apply for waivers and experiences with block scheduling appear in <u>The Four Period Day Network News</u>, a Washington state quarterly publication that began in 1993. This publication invites Washington schools to submit articles that explain their block schedules and the process used to implement and monitor schedules. In-depth studies, however, of schools that have implemented block schedules are limited. In the 1990s, over 10% of Washington schools had implemented some form of block scheduling. Presently, close to 80% of schools in Washington state school districts use some form of block scheduling for some portion of their districts (Chen, 2020). With this percentage of schools making significant changes, research may generate valuable information for those educators who can then use it as part of their decision-making process. Studies that examine changes in schedules offer opportunities for other educators and the general public to see how specific schools handle the process.

This qualitative study examined the process of change for two administrators and ten teachers who had participated in the preparation, planning, and implementation of restructuring through block scheduling. This study endeavors to present more than a surface approach to the process of change. A limited number of studies deal with change in specific areas in school systems, including the following:

<u>The Institutionalization of Change in a Restructured High School: A Case Study</u> (Hoyt, 1996); <u>An Observable Case Study of Issues Related to Site-Based Shared Decision Making</u> (Gonzales, 1994); <u>Restructuring the American High</u>

31

School: A Case Study in California (Guilfoyle, 1994); and A School as a Crucible of Change: A Case Study of Restructuring and a Faculty's Culture (Norwicki, 1992).

The focus of these case studies tends to rest on the restructuring systems schools are using and/or the interactions of stakeholders involved with the change. As case studies, these research presentations do not engage the depth and richness of description involved in the heuristic inquiry, an element I have included in this study. Having participated in all phases of the research, development, and implementation of a block schedule, I have a commitment to this research that a non-participant may not possess.

The school that I chose for this study, Shadle Park High School in Spokane, Washington, selected a different type of block schedule from Kettle Falls High School. This is a large urban school in contrast to Kettle Falls, which is a small rural school. This urban high school has its unique characteristics in the experience of change, its participants' pain and growth, and its collective and individual successes and shortcomings. As this school's staff developed its restructuring plan and moved into block scheduling, its experiences provided a forum for other educators to compare and contrast their own experiences. Sarason (1990) noted that many schools are researching restructuring as they plan changes to their systems. Block scheduling continues to be a choice for many schools in their restructuring process Rettig. (2016). This study adds more information in order to serve schools that are contemplating restructuring and/or researching potential alternatives.

Because systemic qualitative research appears to be limited in this area, I believed the timing was appropriate for this study. With Washington's legislature providing funding to support restructuring efforts through Student Learning Improvement Grants, schools throughout the state applied for grants to make meaningful changes to improve the quality of education. In-depth research of individual educators experiencing the change and being involved in a major restructuring of time through block scheduling provided a succinct view of how change can affect teachers. Regardless of the outcome of the change process, the personal and professional experiences of the people involved in this change process may enrich others who are contemplating change in Washington, as well as in other states. According to Lieberman and Miller (1990), "We must examine the practices of schools engaged in restructuring—looking at nuances, processes, and the ideas that guide them" (p. 761). This study will examine the change process at Shadle Park High School. How the stakeholders, especially the teachers, participate and how they professionally and personally deal with moving to the block schedule of their own design may have important implications for the other people contemplating and experiencing change. My research examined the personal, as well as the professional, results of changing the block schedule. In this study, I concentrated on the journey the teachers made and the effects of the journey on them as they moved toward and participated in the school's restructuring through the block schedule.

Summary

Chapter I has provided the origin and purpose of my study, defining terms unique to the content of later chapters. Included in this section is the background of the restructuring movement of public schools during the decade of the 1990s, an important and substantial beginning of the block schedule becoming a permanent feature of today's educational structure in public schools. The significance of this study centers on the journey the teachers and administrators have experienced and how their professional and personal experiences may enlighten other educators involved in similar change processes.

whwhwhwhwhwhwhwhwhwhwhwhwhwhwhwhwhwhwhwhwhwhwhwhwhwhwhwh

What Happened?

Early Experience in Frustration in Using the Block Schedule

Bill was a holdout, non-supporter of the block schedule, but the rest of the staff voted to move forward and adopt the four-period day format. He stewed in his anger and grief for a while, but he finally decided to voice his concerns to the principal.

"I can't do this, Marie. I can't have my kids blowing horns and pounding drums for 90 minutes! This block stuff just doesn't work for music!" Bill was angry, exhausted, frustrated, and had hit a barrier that he couldn't work through. "There has to be some way to make this work—some other way for music classes."

"There may be some other way. Have a seat, Bill. Let's talk about music." Bill sort of fell into a chair in Marie's office. He had hoped, as principal, she would change the time frame of his classes before he resigned. He was that frustrated.

"Bill, I see you out marching with your band after school. How often do you do that, and how long does that take each time?" Marie asked. "Take your time. Relax." Bill shook his head, then settled into his chair. Marie asked again kindly, "How often? How long?"

"During football season, we practice marching and playing while we march three days a week for about an hour each time. When we practice formations on the field, it takes a couple of additional hours. I usually have them meet on Saturday mornings for two or more hours."

"You also have ensemble practice—solos, duos, trios, quartets—lots of group band practices, as well as your choir practices. You schedule the smaller groups after school, at lunch, before school—right?" Marie continued asking Bill about his use of time.

"Yes. I spend almost as much time after school as you do. And I know you're here a lot of time outside school hours. What's your point?" Bill was settling down emotionally but still a bit wired and wound up.

"I think that you are one of the hardest working teachers I have ever known, Bill. You are working two jobs—one during the day and one after hours and on weekends. I can see why you're, well, frustrated."

"Well, at least you notice. Now you know why this new schedule is killing me."

"What's a good length of time for group band practice in a session?"

"About 40 minutes tops of hard-at-it playing. That's time dedicated just to playing together as a whole band. I like to have them break into instrumental sections as well, especially when we're learning new music," Bill explained.

Marie had written a few notes while Bill talked. "Have you thought about dividing your 90 minute period into sections? On whole band playing days, set up 40 minutes for the whole band, and then follow with sectional or ensemble practices using your practice rooms to separate them?" Marie watched Bill look back with a questioning look. "On clear weather days, why don't you do a whole band playing practice outside at the same time you do marching practice with instruments during your 90 minute class time? While you have them outside, you could also do formation practice on the field some days and strictly marching other days. Could you pre-schedule with PE class so you don't both try to use the same areas at the same time? This could free you up after school. Do you see any possibilities here?"

Bill seemed almost shocked. "Marie, I never thought about any of this. I only thought about doing what I always did, but longer. You mean I can take the kids outside during class for marching practice with instruments? I could have smaller groups practice during class time? Really?" Bill was bursting, rising from his chair. "My God! I've got to think about this."

Marie stopped Bill's departure briefly. "Bill, wait. This whole school-wide change is about using time differently—restructuring. Get creative with your own teaching schedules—and get your life back! If you need help, let me know."

"Thanks, Marie, I came in upset, and I'm leaving ready to figure this out. I just never thought about how to do my job any other way than like I've always done it."

When the opportunity came for teachers to visit other schools with new block schedule changes, Bill requested to join the group. He had put together a reasonable schedule for his music program, compared it with other music teachers, made adjustments as appropriate, and no longer wanted to quit teaching. Best of all, his changes were working well for students and for his own welfare.

What could have happened? Bill could have given up teaching. Marie could have told him to figure it out on his own—other teachers were surviving.

What did happen? Bill chose to look at his schedule differently and make it work for him and for the students he taught. Previously, the music teacher and students were giving up too much after school time. During the semester, Bill gained more students when some bus students found out that they could take music and not stay after school. That was good for students, good for Bill, and good for the music program and the community.

whwhwhwhwhwhwhwhwhwhwhwhwhwhwhwhwhwhwhwhwhwhwhwhwhwhwh

CHAPTER II: REVIEW OF LITERATURE

Effects of Changes in the Workplace, Effect of Change on All Those Who Experienced Change

Chapter I provided an introduction to the change process in schools and how authors of educational studies have recorded the change process of restructuring generally, and more specifically, with block scheduling. Chapter II provides a more in-depth view of the effects on individuals of changes in the workplace, as well as change concerning restructuring in high schools with emphasis on block scheduling as a specific form of restructuring. The four main areas of discussion in this chapter include the following sections:

1. Effects on individuals of changes in the workplace;
2. Reform and restructuring process in high schools;
3. Block scheduling as a form of restructuring and change, with specific examples of the most common forms of block scheduling in high schools;
4. Teachers' professional and personal involvement in change and restructuring.

Finally, a summary presents key ideas and conclusions from the literature review.

Effects on Individuals of Changes in the Workplace

This section develops how changes affect people in the workplace. It discusses the role leaders and managers may hold in facilitating or inhibiting individuals who are in the process of carrying out changes.

How Change Affects People

The participants, recipients of services, and directors of the process of change in organizations may experience varied results. Reflecting upon organizational change, Ford's (1995) comments give an overview of that phenomenon generally applicable to all organizations:

Change in organizations is neither invariably good nor invariably bad, neither progressive nor conservative, neither beneficial nor injurious. Indeed, the effects of change can stray to either extreme in any given situation. One universal I have discovered is that change is always confronted by strong forces holding it in check and sharply circumscribing the capacity of organizations to react to new conditions and opportunities—sometimes with serious results. (p. 4)

Sarason (1983) illustrated the difficulty and confusion that change causes through the following example in the medical field. Sarason explained that patients who had heart attacks two or three decades ago were treated with several weeks of required bed rest for fear that any exertion could lead to another heart attack. Treatment today is dramatically different. Patients are out of bed within a few days. Sarason indicated that both patients and physicians feared change; some physicians refused to change, and some patients were afraid to comply with this dramatic change regardless of factual evidence supporting the change. Through this example, Sarason examined change in practice for any institution. He pointed out that the acceptance of change could not be explained by a certain amount of time passing or the speed at which change was expected to take place. The belief systems of the people who make up the organization, along with their traditions and their culture, have a connection to the success of change. Sarasan stated, "It makes a difference if the change in institutional practice has a voluntary feature, even though that feature may not be free of reluctance or the anxiety engendered by risk-taking or the perception that one has to roll with the punches" (p. 101).

Marris (1974) indicated that people are strongly influenced by their attachments. As some doctors and patients preferred the familiar treatment for heart surgery recovery in Sarason's example above, Marris noted, "Attachment is so central to our security in childhood that it becomes embedded, ineradicably, in the meaning of safety and regard for the rest of our lives" (p. ix). When people experience change and their attachments to familiar patterns of behavior are challenged or severed, Marris indicated that they might become grief-ridden— even if others see the change as essential and good. Marris stated, "Resistance to change is, then, as fundamental an aspect of learning as revision, and adaptability comes as much from our ability to protect the assumptions of experience as our willingness to reconsider them" (p. 16). Marris explained that people seek to predict their own success or failure prior to attempting change or during the change process, and they respond accordingly. If the change is trivial or if it fits into their personal context of meaning, people may adjust easily to the change. If the change is radically different from learned experiences, people may feel unable or unwilling to give up their present continuity, which Marris explained as "a crucial instinct of survival" (p. 17).

Change, as portrayed by both Ford (1995) and Sarason (1983), is characterized by strong forces in opposition that restrict the change process. Information that a certain practice is good may not be enough to bring about major shifts in the way individuals carry out tasks or in the operation of the organization itself. Belief systems may play a role in holding back people involved in change. Changing voluntarily may make the change more palatable, but it does not make it easy, as Sarason explained. Doyle and Doyle (1992) commented on outcomes of change: "Whether an organization fails, plods, or excels, all constituents share in its results" (p. 177). In examining why organizations have difficulty moving individuals or their groups toward change, Ford (1995) explained the attitude of reluctance as follows, "Why gamble an established, imperfect order for the possible disorder . . . It is easier to do nothing than to do something, and inactivity sustains the prevailing, the ordinary and the familiar" (p. 4).

In an effort to meet the organizational needs of a changing market, employees may experience an overload in both their personal and professional lives. Isaacson (1996) addressed the subject of the costs of reform to individuals within organizations. Because of perceived expectations of professional behavior, Isaacson stated that some people feel compelled to accept overloaded conditions, stretching themselves beyond reasonable limits, and, as a result, question their own competencies as professionals.

Bridges (1991) explained that people have to give up their old ways of functioning in organizations before they will be able to embrace change fully. Bridges stated, "Before you can learn a new way of doing things, you have to unlearn the old way . . . change causes the transition, and transition starts with an ending" (p. 19). When change occurs, there is a loss of the old system or pattern. Bridges described the emotional reaction to this loss as a grieving process for those people who are giving up their way of operating and taking on new actions and activities. According to Bridges, when endings take place, people get angry, sad, frightened, depressed, and confused. These emotional states can be mistaken for bad morale, but they aren't. They are *signs of grieving,* the natural sequence of emotions people go through when they lose something that matters to them (p. 24).

What may seem to a group of managers as the most efficient way of operating in their company could cause a considerable amount of emotional turmoil for the people who carry out the new way of operating. The greater the change that is expected of a person, the greater the potential for a negative emotional reaction. As Bridges explained, humans have to give up the old way and grieve its loss before fully accepting a new way of functioning.

Bridges (1980) discussed the ending people experience when facing change and the neutral zone, which he compares to crossing a street. When changing from an old way to a new way, there is a street to cross between the two. During that crossing, a person may analyze what is really happening or changing and how that change is affecting him or her personally and/or professionally. In the neutral zone, a person may give up the old way of doing or being and become willing to move into a new way of doing or being. Bridges stated: Whether it overlaps with the old situation because, inwardly, some ending has already taken place, or whether it overlaps with the new situation because an inner new beginning has not yet been made, the neutral zone is a time of inner orientation (p.130).

Bridges indicated that the neutral zone is a step in the transition from old ways to new ways that are often overlooked. In transition, people may think of the change process, and the people who carry out the change process, as appliances. Once adjusted and plugged into the new change, they will work perfectly. Unfortunately, change does not come that easily or mechanically. Bridges further explained that people are not plug-in items. For people to embrace change, Bridges said that they would need to give up the old ways of operating, grieve the loss of the old ways of operating, transition through the neutral zone, and then make a new beginning.

The issue of change in organizations may need to focus on meeting the needs of individuals within the organizations who are responsible for carrying out changes. Cherniss (1995) described individuals who, as a result of an organization's restructuring requirements, begin to lose their sense of competence. According to Cherniss, people who are expected to do more than they can possibly do with any level of excellence decide to lower their goals from high levels to lower levels, and they may also become less committed to the organization. Cherniss indicated that changes in organizations might create a loss of self-esteem among individuals who do not accept their organization's expectations for them as part of the change. Gardner (1990) noted the importance of a trusting relationship between employees and managers. Gardner explained that employees feel threatened by changes they either do not understand or by expectations they cannot wholeheartedly meet successfully. Trust—if it existed—may erode, leaving people feeling confused, insecure, and/or in a state of anxiety.

Changes that result in individual unrest and anxiety, such as Cherniss (1995), as well as Schaef and Fassel (1958), described for organizations in general, also occur in schools. A historical review of public schools demonstrated that change has been occurring dramatically, paralleling societal changes. Banathy (1991) encouraged educators to do more than maintain the status quo in schools. "In education, it means taking responsibility for designing systems of education that enable and empower future generations to direct their own lives and shape their own destiny" (p. 47). Patterson (1997) indicated that teachers change effectively when their individual self-interests are being met. Patteron stated, "It is natural for employees to choose the safety of being dependent victims of change. It is unnatural for them to choose the ambiguity and risk inherent in being self-accountable as architects shaping how change affects them" (p. 24).

Norum and Lowry (1995) described school restructuring as being emotionally difficult for educators. Classroom teachers are often reluctant to change, and Norum and Lowry pointed out that new paradigms require teachers to give up their usual and comfortable ways of practicing their professions. Teaching in different ways may cause anxiety and fear of failure. The loss of familiar ways of professional delivery of information to students, for example, requires time to grieve the loss and the time to move through the taxes of grief (Norum and Lowry). This process may help teachers let go of past practice in order to allow them to embrace change. Easing the process of change may be the essential key that effective leaders need to apply in order to provide a setting where successful change may occur. Leadership may influence the directions teachers go in either maintaining the status quo or in moving into more acceptance of roles of responsibility.

How Leaders/Leadership Can Be Helpful

Effective leadership may be a component that eases transitional change. Ford (1996) explained, "Excellent leaders are mentors who are committed to excellent communication, to serving, to making sure that conflicts are resolved well. Knowing that groups respond well to their leaders' dynamics, they are aware of their responsibility to be focused, healthy, and courageous" (p. 1). Ford also pointed out that leaders who are ineffective negatively influence others. Guiding people in any organization toward change and growth takes effective leadership skills—it takes an awareness of what the people who are expected to change are going to have to give up to make the change. Change appears to require the willingness to risk, and risk may take place more readily in an atmosphere of trust.

According to Gardner (1990), organizations that have an atmosphere of trust credit, in part, the leadership. Gardner stated, "Leaders can do much to preserve the necessary level of trust" (p. 17). Gardner explained that there are ruthless leaders, such as Hitler and Stalin, who followed Machiavelli's advice about being liars and hypocrites. Gardner contended that "in our society, leaders must work to raise levels of trust" (p. 17). Schaef and Fassel (1988) outlined changes in corporate management; some of the several points they listed for corporate survival include: Organizations have to accept change as a constant and must become less static, that corporate survival cannot be taken for granted, that collegial rule is necessary, that employee involvement is necessary, and that organizations have to move with "the market" and be responsible to the market. (p. 206)

Leadership may provide the support for change by members of an organization through servant leadership, according to Greenleaf (1977). Greenleaf stated: It (servant leadership) will be a role from which oversight is given to a much more fluid arrangement in which leaders and followers change places as many-faceted missions are undertaken and move into phases that call for different deployments of talent. (p.244)

Facilitating change through servant leadership may promote less grieving, and more willingness toward change as the people who carry out change receive active roles and support from leadership they can trust. Greenleaf noted that both leaders and followers in organizations take risks to create change, and the results may relate to trust among participants having a vested interest in the process and outcome. These participants in accepting change are giving up the known for the unknown and, as Bridges (1991) contended, they are experiencing emotional reactions to their loss of the comfortable pattern of operating. A key element in this process is leadership that understands the change process and provides people the opportunity to experience grieving, the neutral zone adjusting, and the beginning of accepting change. Leaders who realize the complexity of change may facilitate the process of guiding constituents through the neutral zone and toward the organization's goals.

The management and leadership in schools are no longer strictly top-down as was once the accepted structure. Teachers, parents, students, and community members are becoming decision-makers in schools. As Scheaf and Fassel (1988) indicated, corporate survival cannot be taken for granted. Competition seems to be developing for public education with other choices, including homeschooling, charter schools, the continued growth of private schools, and other options to traditional public education. Including teachers and others involved in improving schools may provide the impetus for the continued support of education. Leadership in schools may look different in the future from the way it had looked in the past as trends in leadership change (Angus, 1989).

Angus stated, "Leaders are not necessarily those in 'positions of leadership,' and people may exercise leadership or perform an act of leadership on some occasions but not on others" (p. 86). Collegial rule and employee involvement may lead to participants in education becoming involved in leadership in various ways. The transition has occurred from the past pattern of top-down leadership to the more active, involved, and shared leadership many organizations, including schools, are experiencing today. What holds true for organizations in general also has implications for the change process in high schools.

whwhwhwhwhwhwhwhwhwhwhwhwhwhwhwhwhwhwhwhwhwhwhwh

What Happened?

Margaret Chapman and Discrimination

Margaret Chapman was hired to teach English at City High School. Her first two months were difficult, but she was beginning to be more confident in her teaching and her rapport with students. She was also noticing that discrimination toward minority students was considered business as usual, even expected and encouraged. When she sent two students to the office for cheating on a test (same test, same method, same day), she was upset when one was sent back to her class the same period, but the other student was suspended for three weeks. The white student's parents had donated a trampoline to the PE department. The black student, well—no family donations or support within the system. Margaret made a commitment that she would not send any students to the office for consequences again; she would set up her own rules and survive as best she could.

Because Margaret was new to teaching, her classes had more minority students than other English classes in this high school. She created opportunities for dialogue between students of color and white students. At first, this was strained, but in time, black students shared the reality of how integration affected them—their previous school of 500 black students was shut down due to its deplorable condition. That meant their athletic teams were gone. Competing to get on teams in this larger white school of 1,000+ students demonstrated that their chances of participation were slim to none. The administration held one position on the cheer squad for one black student out of eight total. White students thought that was "unfair—why do they get on at all?" When a black student in a "race discussion" in Margaret's room said to the class, "We didn't ask to come here. They tore our old school down. We have to go here. Don't you think we have a right to play sports, be cheerleaders, join clubs? Aren't we students here, too?"

In time, Margaret's students in this class learned to respect one another more than most other people in their community. They asked the hard questions of one another, and they learned to understand how each other felt about discriminatory actions. They didn't always agree, but they listened, asked questions, and began to understand a different point of view.

Margaret was excited to learn that she and her husband were expecting a baby due to be born in September. Her physical shape gave away her condition in the spring. Her students were excited for her, and some of them gave more cooperation than usual. Some students, however, did not. One day in class, a student was using a switchblade to carve his desk. He was slicing rather deeply when Margaret walked near him. As she walked to his desk, she saw the knife, and she told him, "Put away the knife, Jamaul." Margaret kept walking toward the front of the room, but her heart was racing, her hands were sweating, and her mind imagined what Jamaul might do with that knife.

"Will he stab me? Throw the knife? Would any student help me? What if he kills my baby?" As much as she loved her class, this moment brought her intense fear. She was amazed that she was still walking. When she reached her desk, she sat down, facing her class. When her fear subsided enough for her to make eye contact with any students, she looked toward where Jamaul sat. He wasn't at his desk. She wanted to look around, but she was now even more frozen by fear. "Where is he? Where did he go?" she said to herself.

As Margaret tried to stand and look for Jamaul, she turned toward the door. Jamaul came up to her, and held out his arm to support her. "I'm sorry 'bout the blade, Ma'am. I know I shouldn't have it in school or cut stuff."

Margaret, still frightened, received his offer of support. "Thank you, Jamaul. I think I'll just sit down again." Jamaul helped her back to her chair.

"You can have my knife, Ma'am," Jamaul said as he handed her the knife. She saw the knife, blade out, pointing toward her. This, she thought, could be her last moment alive on this earth. "Would anyone in this class help me if he did stab me?" she thought.

"Just put it away, Jamaul. Take it home, and please don't bring it back to school." Of course, the class was watching. Everyone saw Jamaul put the knife in his pocket and sit back at his desk.

What could have happened? Jamaul could have stabbed Mrs. Chapman. She and her baby could have died in front of the class. Or Margaret could have run for the door, and called for help. Police could have arrested Jamaul: for assault with a deadly weapon, attempted murder, or at least armed with a deadly weapon with intent to do bodily harm. The students could have mounted an attack on either the teacher or the student—or both. Many people could have been hurt or worse. Jamaul could have gone to prison. Margaret could have shared this incident with the administration, but based on the way administrators handled discipline, especially for black students, she believed that she couldn't risk what would happen to this student if she did write up this incident.

What did happen? Jamaul put the knife away. Margaret told the students that they should not bring weapons to class, Jamaul understood that, and Jamaul promised the class and the teacher that he would never bring them again. One of the more outspoken students said, "I think this whole situation should be for just our class to know about. Can we keep this right here so it doesn't turn out bad for anyone?" The students seemed to accept that idea. Jamaul could be arrested. The teacher could get fired.

Margaret did not write up Jamaul for having a knife. She believed that he would be expelled if she turned this into the office. She did not teach the next year due to having a healthy baby in September.

Jamaul did not bring his knife to school—or at least no one saw him with a knife. He graduated from high school and enlisted in the Marines, serving honorably for 30+ years.

How does this relate to *Educating Humanely Applied?* Discriminatory behavior does not serve students or staff well. Neither the teacher nor the students felt safe, protected, or comfortable sharing any of this incident with the administration based on the way administrators exhibited prejudice and issued consequences to students. Trust is paramount in building relationships, teaching students, and providing a safe learning environment.

whwhwhwhwhwhwhwhwhwhwhwhwhwhwhwhwhwhwhwhwhwhwhwhwhwh

Educators' Experiences with Changes in High Schools

This section provides several definitions of change and restructuring as high schools attempt new ways to upgrade the quality of teaching and learning. Whatever the restructuring method schools employ, their common goals target improving learning for students, which, in turn, challenges the way teachers teach. The challenge of changing for teachers is an essential element of this portion of the chapter.

Change Defined

Change in high schools to improve climate, culture, and achievement has become a concern throughout the 20th century and has become a stronger effort since the Commission on Excellence in Education delivered the report <u>A Nation at Risk</u> (Commission on Excellence in Education, 1983) to the public. This report describes the high rate of functional illiteracy among adults, the unfavorable comparison of our students' standardized test scores with other nations, and the high rate of illiteracy among minority youth (up to 40%). These topics were only some of the areas brought to the nation's attention through this report (pp. 8-9). In response to the national report, more public attention became focused on education and what changes might bring out improvements.

Lewis (1998) listed several definitions of educational restructuring and/or change from renowned educators:

Frank Newman, president of the Education Commission of the States, explains, "Restructuring means changing the nature of schools from the interior so that students become active learners, partners in the learning process." (p. 3)

"Education is what teachers do," says Harvard University researcher Eleanor Duckworth. "If policy is to affect students' experiences in schools, it must be through what teachers do, how they do it, and what it means to them." (p. 3)

American Federation of Teachers' former President Albert Shanker states, "Restructuring is different. It seeks to create new relationships for children and teachers. . . . [it] is about the dynamics of learning. It focuses on the essentials— on collaboration and on problem-solving. (pp. 3-4)

These definitions represent only a fraction of the many definitions of restructuring in the literature on educational change. Because many definitions of change also exist, it follows that the results of change and restructuring may also be multifaceted. According to Lieberman, Darling-Hammond, and Zuckerman (1991), change is not an easy process, and generally, when a school system decides to change in a major way, conflict among educators may develop as a normal part of the process. Miles and Huberman (1984) contended that as much as people who are intent upon making a change would like other participants to accept the process wholeheartedly, change often takes place in practice before people begin to adopt the reasons for the change as part of their own belief systems. Greenleaf (1977) defined change as constant. He stated, "[But] it is in constant change and growth alone that life can be grasped at all . . . change is natural movement . . ." (p. 173). Bridges (1991) described change as situational: "*Change* is situational: the new site, the new boss, the new team roles, the new policy. *Transition* is the psychological process people go through to come to terms with a new situation. Change is external, transition is internal" (p. 3).

Of particular interest to the current study are the work of Hord, Rutherford, Huling-Austin, and Hall (1987) at the Research and Development Center for Teacher Education (R&DCTE) at the University of Texas, Austin campus. This federally funded research focused not on "what schools should do . . . What we were about was an unflinching pursuit to learn about the school improvement *process;* what it is, whom it involves, what are its effects, and how it might be managed" (Hord et al., p. 4). When school districts receive, for example, a new math series, Hord et al. pointed out that the boxes of books and materials distributed to math teachers will not ensure that the program will be implemented. The authors developed the Concerns-Based Adoption Model (CBAM). This model contains the following conclusions:

1. Change is a process, not an event.
2. Change is accomplished by individuals.
3. Change is a highly personal experience.
4. Change involves developmental growth.
5. Change is best understood in operational terms.

6. The focus of facilitation should be on individuals, innovations, and the context. (pp. 5-6)

Hord (1987) also discussed all of these aspects of change. In an explanation of the first conclusion, she indicated that change is not the program itself but the "process occurring over time" (p. 93). Adopting a block schedule is an event, but making the schedule a successful working entity is a process that takes many years. Hord explained the second conclusion, "Change is accomplished by individuals," by noting that change, when viewed as a program or event, is impersonal. Hord stated, "Only when a sufficient number of individuals have genuinely embraced change can it truly be said that the institution or system has changed" (p. 94).

The following quote is Hord's (1987) description of the third conclusion: "Change is a highly personal experience . . . . Too often individuals may be viewed as a numerical assemblage of largely interchangeable units, with little allowance made for differences in how they will respond. Though they are approached individually, they are expected to behave, in effect, collectively. This approach does grave injustice to the staggering diversity and alternately wonderful and maddening unpredictability of human behavior; it also seriously undermines the likelihood of successful implementation. (p. 94)

Hord (1987) noted, in the fourth conclusion, that change "is an irregular assemblage of emotional, intellectual, and behavioral responses that affect the individual and thus, the school, in a variety of ways" (p. 94). According to Hord, individuals experience a change in their own way and at their own rate, uniquely developing in emotional stages and skill levels. This is an individual process with teachers having a variety of emotional reactions, learning to apply new training and skills at various levels of expertise. Administrators and evaluators who realize this may find less frustration and more understanding in assessing both individual and system progress.

The fifth conclusion may be the area where communication is most critical between the administrators and the teachers in school change. "Change is best understood in operational terms" (p. 96), according to Hord (1987), who explained that teachers need to know clearly what this change will require of them individually and collectively. Will they need training? If so, how much training? How will this change affect the students and the general organization of the classroom? When leaders of change explain in a timely manner how this change will actually affect the individual teachers and students, their communication may reduce anxiety and resistance for many participants.

The final conclusion, "The focus of facilitation should be on individuals, innovations, and the context" Hord et al., 1987, p. 6), tends to be the opposite of how people generally view change. Educators may see, for example, the schedule or the curriculum as the change when, in fact, Hard et al. noted, "Only people can make change by altering their behavior" (p. 6). As the process develops, individuals and their reactions to change may cause variations in timetables and plans. In a faculty of 200 teachers or 5 teachers, every individual teacher may affect the whole process and the final results.

Restructuring in Schools and Its Effect on Educators

Lewis (1989) observed, "Like the proverbial blind men trying to describe an elephant, educators who feel around for a definition of the latest stage in the reform of schools—restructuring—see the situation differently" (p. 1). According to Glickman (1993), "School people are often caught unwittingly in structures and conventions that are counterproductive to the improvement of teaching practice" (p. 21). Glickman explained that people are unable to make their present schools work better, and the energy level required to make change produces discouragement and insecurity. The change process tends to be successful when the people who will be carrying out the change and the people whom the change is affecting have some level of involvement in the planning process; however, as Glickman pointed out, change is still painful for some participants.

Bolman and Deal (1984) stated that reorganization or restructuring efforts can be painful for some participants. When people cannot express themselves individually and creatively, Bolman and Deal noted that organizations become inefficient. If change is mandated upon people who do not understand or accept the process or the reasons for the change, conflict may become entrenched, and the change may simply not happen as planned, or it may not happen at all. Fullan (1991) pointed out that when individuals perceive that they are struggling with the expectations set for them or those they set for themselves, their responses could include overworking themselves to the point of exhaustion; trying but then giving up; or simply giving up at the outset without comment or admission.

In a two-stage quantitative and qualitative study on teacher attitudes, Ruscoe and Whitord (1991) indicated that teachers expressed positive experiences in their restructuring process when they had a supportive administration, shared decision-making, colleagues willing to participate in change, and a student-centered environment. Teacher attitudes were measured through a series of surveys, the first of which included: nine demographic questions and 73 attitudinal items. Based on results from this survey and from interviews with teachers, the 1989 version was revised to include four demographic questions and 61 attitudinal questions focusing on efficacy, learning climate, and empowerment. The 1989 survey form was used again in 1990. (p. 2)

This survey includes 949 teachers in 24 development schools. The interview portion of this study specifically indicated the importance teachers placed on the leadership of their principals. Teachers expressed that their principals allowed freedom, the right to try new ideas without fear of failure and encouraged communication of ideas, fears, problems, and suggestions. Support from school leaders, according to this study, provided teachers the inspiration they needed to participate in the various restructuring programs.

Klecker and Loadman (1996), in a quantitative study of principals' openness to change in 168 restructuring schools, showed that principals who participated in the study did not show a high level of agreement with the changes restructuring was bringing to their schools. Generally, however, the principals indicated that benefits would come from the changes, and they were willing to facilitate the changes in their schools. This study demonstrated a high correlation between the administrators' behavior in carrying out restructuring plans with their cognitive belief that the restructuring process would positively improve student performance. When principals believe a change is positive, their support may make a difference in the success of change. The reverse may also be true in that lack of principal support could significantly reduce the success of a change. Schools where principals are convinced that a restructuring plan is going to improve student performance, even if the principals do not care for the plan, may have a greater opportunity for success than in schools where principals do not believe the restructuring plan will improve student performance.

Hord et al. (1987) developed the concept of Innovation Configurations (IC) to assist principals responsible for monitoring teachers in the process of change. Hord et al. referred to principals and others whose roles were to evaluate teachers and their progress in applying innovations to their classes as "change facilitators" (p. 54). With IC checklists as guides, change facilitators monitor the number and variety of materials teachers use with children, teachers' individual diagnosis of each student's performance, record keeping, teaching techniques, the grouping of children, and the individual attention a teacher allots per pupil.

Hord et al. (1987), through an evaluation system called "Stages of Concern (SoC)" (p. 31), provided three dimensions with seven levels, or stages, directed toward facilitators (principals and others actively helping to bring about an innovation), that offered both external evaluation and self-evaluation for teachers experiencing change. Hord et al. indicated that "the developmental nature of concerns is further reflected in three dimensions—self, task, and impact—into which the seven stages may be grouped" (p. 30).

Hall and Hold (1987) provided definitions for the three dimensions and the seven stages. (I have underlined Hall and Hord's arms for dimensions and stages.) The dimension of self begins with awareness. At this level, a person is not focused on the direction of any change. The next level is informational. A person becomes interested in innovation and wants to know more about it. The person does not picture himself or herself involved in the innovation. The third stage in the dimension of self is personal. At this stage, people question their abilities to make a change. They may lack self-confidence, as well as confidence in the support of other people connected to this innovation—administrators, school board members, students, parents, some faculty members, and the community.

The next dimension, task, has one stage: management. Hall and Hold (1987) indicate that the focus on this stage includes all aspects of how to make the change become a working reality. People consider training, materials, resources, funding, and others involved in managing the innovation as competently as possible.

Impact, the final dimension, includes consequence, collaboration, and refocusing. Hall and Hord defined consequence as the stage where people try to improve their own ability to meet the requirements of successful change. Looking at how the innovation is affecting others and according to Hall and Hord, "Expanding his/her facility and style for facilitating change is also the focus" (p. 224). Hall and Hord (1987) defined collaboration as follows: "Coordinating with other change facilitators and /or administrators to increase one's capacity in facilitating the use of innovation is the focus. Increased coordination and communication for increased effectiveness of the innovation are the focus. Issues related to involving other leaders in support of and facilitating the use of the innovation for increased impact are indicated." (p. 224)

The final stage in the dimension of impact is refocusing. Change facilitators look for ways to improve upon the change or innovation and to find alternatives that may increase positive results for everyone involved. Having a tangible guide, such as Hall and Hord's (1987) Stages of Concern and Levels of Use, to monitor change processes may provide principals and teachers with a way to communicate their progress, if progress occurs, and evaluate its impact on teaching and learning, giving participants a more accurate perspective of their participation and results.

According to Fullan (1991), organizations involved in change, and individuals within organizations do not view change in its full perspective. Fullan stated: Change is not conceived of as being multidimensional . . . Ignorance of these dimensions explains a number of interesting phenomena in the field of educational change: for example, why some people accept an innovation they do not understand; why some aspects of change are implemented, and others not; and why strategies for change neglect certain components. (p 36)

Fullan contended that the individuals within an organization accept changes in a variety of degrees of acceptance. Some people will respond to change without understanding or questioning their roles or the process. Other people will do all that they can to prevent the change from happening, even when the change has proven to be a better way of operating for the organization and for the individuals involved. In some cases, leadership may lead and encourage others to lead within the change process.

In other cases, leadership may be part of the confusion, and the change process does not become effective. Fullan outlined three dimensions that change introduces into a school system: "(1) . . . the possible use of new or revised materials (direct instructional resources such as curriculum materials or technologies), (2) the possible use of new teaching approaches (i.e., new teaching strategies or activities), and (3) the possible alteration of beliefs (e.g., pedagogical assumptions and theories underlying particular new policies or programs." (p. 37)

Fullan's dimensions give insight into the expectations that change may be thrusting upon teachers which could be overlooked in the process of changing a schedule time frame. Teachers who move from a traditional 50-minute teaching period after functioning in that time frame for many years may fear or resent the changes they may have to make in their delivery of information. For example, a teacher who has lectured in the 50-minute period schedule may find that he or she is unable to continue that delivery system for a longer block of 100 or 150 minutes on a daily basis. The lecturing teacher may need to invoke different teaching materials that are unfamiliar to him or her. Changing from a teacher-centered approach to presenting information to a student-centered approach may cause inner conflict about teaching itself. The lecturing teacher who has been the center of learning may struggle to give that position to students through both individual and group assignments. The lecturing teacher may even feel this change is unethical and a breach of performing the job of a teacher.

Fullan (1993) made a strong case for the essential role of the teacher in the change process. He indicated that principals need to provide teachers with training to become leaders and, as a result, extend the leadership responsibilities beyond the principalship. Fullan stated that Principals need to help create the conditions and capacity for every teacher to become a leader. It sounds ideal, but teaching will not become a learning profession until the vast majority of its members become (in my terms) change agents capable of working on their own sense of purpose through inquiry, competence building, and collaboration. (p. 127)

Fullan indicated that change would simply not occur if teachers do not make it happen. When teachers are involved, directed, and self-directed toward the change process, and when they are actively involved in leadership roles in carrying out change, schools will experience success in reaching their goals for change.

Once a change process is enacted in schools, some teachers still may not be able to imagine teaching differently from the way they were taught or the way they have been teaching. Fine (1994) indicated that teachers' comfort zones might be seriously challenged, and they may be unsure or perhaps not ready to attempt to change. Many teachers and administrators appear ready to make changes in the way they provide for their students' education. Teams of teachers with competent administrators and interested parents and community members are working together to make a positive difference in their schools. Fine pointed out that trying harder to improve schools nationally is a common theme in schools across the nation.

Trying harder is admirable, but Darling-Hammond (1995) indicated that trying harder may not be enough. Darling-Hammond noted that "rather than just trying harder, schools are reinventing teaching and learning, roles and responsibilities, and relationships with parents and communities, so that they can help a greater range of students learn more powerfully and productively" (p. 157). The process of reinventing teaching and learning, as Darling-Hammond stated, is bringing about changes in public education. Examining the change process itself, and as Bridges (1991) described, the transition process that happens when change is introduced may contribute to stressful change. Trying hard may indicate a positive attitude about change, but the people in transition need to let go of the old ways of operating and grieve the loss before they can assimilate the new change in the system and in themselves as part of the system.

High school restructuring has caused many teachers to look at teaching differently. For high school teachers, the one area of reforming American high schools through changing to block scheduling has caused change in their professional lives and personal values about teaching. Adjusting the daily schedule from the traditional schedule to a block schedule, according to Dooley (1992), has changed learning from "the quiet concept" (p. 14) of the lecture-based classroom as the epitome of the best classroom environment for learning. Dooley contended, "The need for learning to be an active, dynamic process is well-documented and rationalized in current educational literature . . . [teachers are] formulating new relationships . . . between students and teachers, students and students, teachers and parents, and students and parents" (p. 14). The change in relationships and the change in teaching is not an automatic, easy shift for many of the teachers involved in secondary education. In discussing reforming and restructuring high schools, an appreciation of Fullan's (1991) research on the emotional impact of change may enlighten individuals and organizations in the midst of change. Reform and restructuring are changes in public education that touch the lives of many people in deeply emotional ways. Losing track of that impact, especially upon the teachers who carry much of the responsibility for changing, may reduce the success of positive change in education.

The goal of current reform and restructure planning, according to Sizer (1992), is to teach students how to think. Sizer developed the Coalition of Essential Schools, an organization housed at Brown University that has been involved in changing schools that seek help and guidance in restructuring. According to Kadel (1994), more than 50 schools are part of this coalition which assists "schools in improving climate, culture and redesigning approaches to student learning and achievement" (p. 13).

Block Scheduling

This section presents general information about block scheduling as one of the restructuring methods employed in school systems. In 1998, an ERIC query on the block schedule turned up 57 entrees. These 57 entrees offer a variety of approaches to the topic of scheduling. This section also presents other sources which provide the rationale for considering block scheduling. The effects of using time differently through adjustments in the schedule, according to several educational writers included in this section, may have a major impact on the way teachers teach and the way students learn.

Educational Resources Information Center (ERIC) Search of the Block Schedule

An ERIC query of 57 articles and studies on block scheduling included many facets of this topic. Several articles and studies introduced block schedules in a general sense, comparing blocks to traditional schedules and/or explaining characteristics of both positive and negative impacts on the people involved (Canady and Retting, 1993, 1995; Munroe, 1989; Phillips, 1997, Rettig and Canady, 1996; Shortt and Thayer, 1997).

A number of articles and studies in this search related to specific subject areas. For example, Day and Binkley (1996) noted the importance of science teachers being trained prior to teaching in a 90-minute or longer block. Gerking (1995) targeted the advantages of teaching science over a longer period and suggested teaching activities. The National Science Teachers Association (1997) provided a collection of articles that included strategies for teaching in the longer block. Shockey (1997) produced a quantitative and qualitative study involving student retention in mathematics due to the change to a block format. He concentrated on pre-, mid-, and post-tests of precalculus students, finding no significant differences in retention intervals using block scheduling.

North Carolina State Department of Public Instruction (1996) provided a guide to address foreign language teaching and learning results in block schedule settings. This guide contains specially designed formats for block schedules for language classes, along with samples of Spanish and French curriculum guides providing assistance to foreign language teachers. "A Report of the Task Force on Block Scheduling by the Wisconsin Association of Foreign Language Teachers" (1995) addressed foreign language teaching in 11 schools with a concentration on student learning, teacher and student workloads, and the need to modify methods and student assessment. L. Reid (1995) addressed teachers' and students' perceptions of their success in teaching and learning English skills. L. Reid also provided a list of questions to use to evaluate a block schedule. Claxton and Bryant (1996) discussed the advantages of physical education instruction and provided a sample lesson plan for a 90-minute physical education class.

In addition to individual subjects, some articles focused on individual high school programs in general areas where block scheduling is applied. Zaragoza (1997) noted the positive effect the block had on teaching nonnative English speaking students. Block scheduling is only one of 14 areas Zaragoza developed in this article. Syropoulow (1996) indicated positive results in block scheduling for at-risk ninth graders. He used standardized test scores and attendance records as part of his comparative study of ninth-grade students' improvements with block scheduling. Fitzgerald (1996) targeted brain-compatible teaching in the block and recommended strategies and activities that capture students' attention and interest. Geismar and Pullease (1996) studied the trimester combined with block scheduling, and they examined students' achievement on standardized test scores to measure students' levels of success.

Two articles in this ERIC search noted that the year-round school plan and block scheduling were used together. Bradford (1996) described an 8-credits-per-year plan with students concentrating on two courses each six-week period. Gee (1997) found that combining the block schedule with the year-round school year did not increase the financial burden of the district.

Tadlock and Barrett-Roberts (1995) and Hackman (1995) included block scheduling as one of many areas in middle school education. Rettig and Canady (1995) addressed the elementary education concern of blocking specialists who provide music, art, physical education, and other enrichment lessons into the elementary students' schedule in effective ways for classroom teachers. Neither of these areas has a direct effect on high school block scheduling, with the exception of schools that share teachers in their middle and elementary school classes.

The ERIC search noted many studies and articles which explained a single school's experience with block schooling. Cresswell and Rasmussen (1996), Guskey and Kifer (1995), Kruze and Zulkoski (1997), Mistretta and Polansky (1997), Snyder (1997), Spencer and Lowe (1994), West (1996), and Wilson (1995), presented one school's experiences with adopting and adapting to a variety of forms of the block schedule.

Davis-Wiley, George, and Mozart (1995) developed a quantitative and qualitative study of two schools. Through a survey and interviews, Davis-Wiley et al. examined the effect the change process had on teachers and administrators. Terms including "tiring," "hectic," "stressful," and "exhausting" (p. 12) appeared on teachers' survey forms, but no in-depth study of teachers' emotional reactions was developed. Fletcher (1997) examined six schools through questionnaire responses, and Pisapia and Westfall (1997a) studied the effects schedules in five schools had on teaching strategies and student performance. Pisapia and Westfall used a survey format to gather information from teachers in five schools.

Thomas and O'Connell (1997a) and Pisapia and Westfall (1997b) concentrated on parent perceptions of block scheduling. Hurley (1997a), Thomas and O'Connell (1997b), and Pisapia and Westfall (1997a and b) also wrote reports which gave student perceptions of the block schedule. These articles included information about student achievement and behavior, as well as students' opinions. Whitla, Bempechat, Perrone, and Carroll (1992) described a two-year pilot program that was discontinued in spite of positive results. The school district had both a block schedule program and a traditional program at the same time. Financial problems and lack of community support, along with inner conflict among the teachers from the two programs, contributed to the discontinuation of the block schedule.

Studies on Educators' Experiences with Alternative Schedules

Few of the articles in the ERIC search relate specifically to teachers' personal and emotional experiences as they participated in the block schedule. Pisapia (1997c), through a survey, compared and contrasted teachers' perceptions of the block schedule and the traditional schedule. Hurley (1997b) concentrated on teachers' attitudes through interviews of teachers in academic and vocational areas. Hurley noted,

Some conditions that are advantageous to some teachers are a disadvantage to others. This is to be expected; high school teachers' situations differ greatly depending on their discipline. Furthermore, high school faculty and cultures vary greatly. In some schools, math teachers are influential; in other schools, vocational and fine arts teachers exercise informal influence. And influential teachers can be powerful shapers of school opinion. (p. 61).

Bruckner (1997) targeted teachers' frustrations, stress, and classroom concerns. Bruckner noted that problems that existed prior to the block schedule's inception, such as poor attendance and students' lack of achievement, were attributed to the block schedule. According to Bruckner, "School leaders may decree that a change will occur, but no one but the individual teacher will make that happen in the classroom" (p. 52).

Irmsher (1996b) gave general information about block scheduling and an account of Oregon schools involved in this change. Within this study, Irmsher noted that in one school, "they (teachers) became angry and hostile. Many are still bitter, and the principal who initiated the change has moved on" (p. 15). Although the emotional involvement of teachers is limited in this study, Irmsher's list of suggestions to make a successful change to block scheduling may assist any school considering this form of schedule. Items in this list include paying teachers for additional time to learn, hiring substitutes to give teachers time for preparation, and reducing the number of classes per teacher. Irmsher (1996a) also noted that change is painful. She pointed out that mandating a change of schedule does not ensure success.

Rationale for Considering Block Scheduling

According to Carroll (1989), the block schedule provides a frame of time that can bring about a variety of delivery systems that will be more consistent with students' varied learning styles. Staff development programs that deal with delivery systems and learning styles may help teachers learn new ways to teach. Carroll shared that quality training may assist teachers who want to lift the quality of education in their schools. The block schedule, in its many forms, is finding success in schools where districts provide financial support in the form of staff development programs, materials, and compensation for teachers' time (Irmsher, 1996a). Students' time may be used more valuably, regardless of the scheduling format, with quality training for teachers (Anderson, 1993). The block schedule has some positive ways to maintain academic learning time that teacher training facilitates.

Academic learning time was a focus for Anderson (1993) in her research on how schools use time in scheduling students. Anderson prepared an extensive study for the National Association of Secondary School Principals on time and its use, as well as its misuse, in public schools. As part of the research, Anderson spent time in public schools and recorded how time was used by students each day. Anderson charted academic learning time, that is, time actually spent with course content material, at 41% of the actual learning time in the school day. Students averaged being on task 62%, with 83% of the school day designated as actual instructional time or time in classes. Teachers had the opportunity to actively present or monitor student learning activities. According to Anderson, "A critical difference exists between the measure of time (how we tell time) and the meaning of time (what time tells us)" (p. 18).

Kane (1994), in her report for the National Education Commission on Time and Learning, stated that Time is the missing element in our great national debate about learning and the need for higher standards for all students. Our schools and the people involved with them—students, administrators, parents, and staff—we are prisoners of time, captives of the school clock and calendar. We have been asking the impossible of students—that they learn as much as their foreign peers while spending only half as much time in core academic subjects. The reform movement of the last decade is destined to flounder unless it is harnessed to more time for learning. (p. 7)

Kane compared America's time commitment toward education to that of other nations, and she reported that our students attend school for less than half the amount of time than students in Japan, France, and Germany attend. Kane explained that American students spend less time in academic classes because their schedules include drivers' education, vocational classes, and many other elective, non-academic classes. Kane pointed out that American students are packaged together or scheduled into six or seven learning periods of 45 to 50 minutes per day. As a result, gifted students who need less time to absorb material are essentially held back from learning opportunities, and students who need more time to learn do not get the teacher attention they need and, as a result, are continually behind. Kane recommended that by examining what teachers are teaching, how long they are teaching, and how our schools are organized, it may be possible to correct the negative results of our educational system. Other recommendations from this study include, "Use time in different ways, keep the school open longer to meet the needs of children and communities, give teachers the time they need . . . share the responsibility—finger-pointing and evasion must end" (p. 7).

Using time differently is the main idea of block scheduling. By organizing the school day in blocks of time that allow teachers the time to use a variety of teaching styles which, in turn, accommodate student learning styles, our teachers may be able to meet more effectively the needs of students. Blocks of time within the school day and following the school day or during the traditional summer vacation may provide options that benefit students, the community, and the overall improvement of education. As Kane indicated, finger-pointing, or indicating a fault in one another for the failure to measure up to a variety of standards needs to stop. The energies of educators may be better spent on problem-solving rather than problem blaming.

Kane pointed out that teachers in the traditional six, seven, or eight periods per day of instruction meet with too many students, teach too many sections, and often teach too many subjects per day to be able to do an effective job of reaching students, establishing rapport with students and parents, and maintaining professional growth through additional training and professional enrichment. The traditional schedule is also referred to as the factory model, a process analogous to the assembly line operation in companies. The students in this analogy may be on a conveyor belt, getting a part of their education at one station, moving on to the next station (class) or another part, and so on throughout the school day and the school year. At the end of the process, the students are considered ready to enter into society simply because they followed the process and took their place on the educational conveyor belt—a timed process that is equated with a complete education. Schools may be able to use time more effectively in educating students.

Using time differently has been part of the vision of many school districts as they restructure their school programs. One of the most well-known programs that use blocks of time differently from the traditional seven-period day is the Copernican Plan. Singh (1992) explained that the Copernican Plan, using a block schedule, was instituted by Joseph Carroll (1989) as a means of providing more manageable workloads for both teachers and students. This plan provided blocks of two classes per day for 60 days to complete two credits. Carroll also wanted to encourage students who had dropped out of school to come back. Being able to complete a minimum number of credits in 60 days instead of 180 days was a powerful incentive. Carroll pointed out that team teaching could help less-skilled teachers learn from more competent teachers in the longer blocks to provide a better learning situation for students.

Stemnock (1975) prepared a study in regard to the four-day-per-week schedule with a block format and listed several reasons for its development in the schools where she researched. Blocking classes into four days for longer periods of time alleviated overcrowding and seeded financially in areas of heating, transportation, electricity, and other areas. It gave learning opportunities outside the classroom. Part of this program included school-to-work programs and athletic schedules on the fifth day and weekends to alleviate time out of academic classes on the other four days per week. This study described the four-day plan in three districts. Stemnock also reported on the Lockenmeyer Plan, a six-day-per-week plan with 75% of the students attending four days per week at any particular time. General results indicated that students with lower achievement in longer periods maintained consistent grades with the previous year's grades, indicating no benefit but no loss. Students in the first year of the lengthened period did not improve. However, where enrichment activities are intermixed with academic activities, achievement improves.

Stemnock pointed out that the time frame of the blocks is not the final determinant of success or failure; the quality of instruction will have more effect on the measure of academic success than the block itself. Stemnock's report indicated that schools open for the four-day week saved the districts financially. Stemnock noted, however, that the variety of learning opportunities seemed more beneficial to students in a five-day-per-week program.

According to Singh (1992), block scheduling has become a vehicle to restructure schools because educators could see the potential for improving the total school program in the larger time period. From the point of view of teachers, larger blocks of time per day meant meeting with smaller numbers of students per day. The smaller numbers of students meant more opportunities for quality time with students each day. The reverse is also true: students would meet the standards each day for fewer teachers. This presented opportunities that could reduce stress for both students and teachers. Reduced stress leads to more effective learning and a reduction in behavior problems.

Stuck and Wyne (1982) indicated that teachers needed to reduce transition time between tasks, minimize ineffective use of nonproductive time, especially by beginning and ending lessons on time, and closely monitor student learning. Perhaps if teachers had fewer blocks of learning to present daily and met with fewer students daily, they might have a greater opportunity to carry out these improvements. Stuck and Wyne's ideas seemed more possible with adjustments in a traditional schedule or with block scheduling.

Omak, Washington's high school restructuring (Neimeyer, 1992) indicated that record-keeping duties were reduced in several areas. Attendance for four periods per day was easier to track than for their previous seven-period day. This held true for the teachers in classrooms, as well as the main office requirements. Although each student may have more grades in a class period, teachers charted fewer students each day and each half of the school year. Teachers each had three classes per one-half year or semester. Record keeping in the form of keeping track of classwork and homework was also reduced for students who participated in four classes per semester and who had only four classes of coursework and homework to deal with each day. Among their four classes, students usually had two or three academic classes and one or two non-academic classes or classes requiring a minimal amount of out-of-class work, such as physical education or woodworking classes. With students passing fewer times in the hallways, behavior record keeping was also reduced because students had fewer opportunities to get involved in conflicts among themselves in the less structured environment of the hallways. When breaks occurred, they were longer and less rushed than the shorter passing time allowed in the traditional seven-period schedule.

The block schedule in Omak (Neimeyer, 1992) included a ten-minute break at which time high school students could eat breakfast. The principal attributed fewer behavior problems among students who ate nutritious food during the mid-morning break. Students who were hungry tended to respond in a variety of ways—in a lethargic, irritable, or unfriendly manner. Students who had breakfast seemed more attentive and interested in participating in classes.

Negative impacts also arose in block scheduling for Omak High School. Teachers indicated that they had a much more complex situation in preparing for classes. Planning for a 90- or 120-minute period with the same set of students presented teachers with the requirement of changing the way they delivered material. In the past, the majority of the Omak High School teachers had used the lecture delivery method. Lecturing for 90 minutes or more could be difficult for some teachers to prepare and deliver, as well as for students to receive, remember, and apply (Neimeyer, 1992). Kane (1994) discussed the importance of providing teachers time for training to learn new delivery methods. Without training, changing teaching style may become a barrier to teachers who have difficulty with the use of the longer time frame. W. Reid (1995) stressed the importance of having a strong staff development program that teachers strongly support. Introducing teachers to ways to deliver information through training may alleviate anxiety in teachers, as well as their students.

Block scheduling may offer various ways for schools to arrange time in segments that offer different solutions to meet the needs of students and teachers. With time through block scheduling becoming a flexible component instead of fixed permanently in the traditional seven-period day, schools may have opened additional opportunities to those available in the traditional schedule. English (1993) pointed out that by opening up scheduling opportunities, the school boundaries may include community and county services and agencies (e.g., libraries, museums, hospitals, social services agencies, and businesses). Opportunities may be vast for schools that are interested in bringing these types of programs into their schools. Both traditional and block schedules may incorporate these programs into their schedules. Some beneficial opportunities may be present for schools interested in reviewing their mission, continuing to center their schools with students as their primary concern, and when planning innovations or change, involving the major participants in a multifaceted program (English, 1993). Block scheduling is one way to provide flexibility to incorporate programs and use time differently and effectively.

Experiences of Teachers' and Administrators' Involvement in School Restructuring

This section presents literature regarding the roles of the teachers and administrators in restructuring, in designing and carrying out the plans for reform, and in determining the success of the plans. Teachers' emotional involvement and their reactions to change, as several educational writers indicate, may have strong professional and personal impact upon their abilities to adjust to change.

Because teachers tend to carry out many aspects of restructuring, they may be instrumental in developing and implementing the process of change. Derrington (1998), a proponent of collaborative leadership, said that principals as school leaders can best serve their teaching staff by empowering members of their staffs to take on leadership roles from the beginning of any reform or restructuring ideology. Derrington further explained that when teachers become partners with principals in the change process, the foundation for effective change is in place. Leiberman (1995) stated, "Principals do not control, but, rather, support teachers, helping to create opportunities for them to grow and develop" (p. 9). According to Leiberman and Miller (1990), effective change for teachers can take place when teachers experience "leadership. a shared mission, school goals, necessary resources, the promotion of colleagueship, and the provision of professional growth opportunities for teachers" (p. 761). Counselors also play a major role in the change process. Their efforts with students and staff help, or hinder, the change process, especially when principals push control at all costs.

whwhwhwhwhwhwhwhwhwhwhwhwhwhwhwhwhwhwhwhwhwhwhwhwh

What Happened?

Counselor/Principal Relations by Jenny Rose

Background: Kelsey had been an elementary school counselor for 8 years. A counselor position became open in her husband's (who was also a counselor) district. Kelsey accepted the job. Throughout Kelsey's 8 years of working as a counselor in a couple of high poverty elementary schools, she had always received excellent evaluations. Her heart and soul were part of working with very special young children, and she LOVED her job. Because there were so many students with high needs at Kelsey's school, especially homeless families – she worked beyond the daily hours to help these families that she came to know and love. It was not unusual to see Kelsey working on the weekends.

What did happen? There was no interview process between the principal and Kelsey to see if she would be a good fit as a counselor in this new school, new district. Kelsey was just placed there. The principal, Ms. Brown, had been at this school for six years and had problems with counselors before Kelsey. Ms. Brown had developed some practices that previous counselors had issues with, such as asking counselors to "spy" on certain staff members and report back to her. Rarely did a counselor last a year before asking to be transferred somewhere else. Kelsey managed to get through the first half of the school year, but she became increasingly anxious with all of Ms. Brown's practices and demands. She sought help from her local teacher's union, but Ms. Brown would deny accusations when questioned by the school district. It was basically Kelsey's word against Ms. Brown's word.

Around January is when things began to get even worse. Ms. Brown started questioning Kelsey's involvement with a young student, Lea, who was living with her aunt and had been through a lot of traumas. Kelsey had taken Lea "under her wing" and was making sure that Lea had clean clothes, driving Lea to outside counseling, making sure she had enough food at home, having Lea spend time with Kelsey's family, and so much more. This was all with the approval of the aunt, who didn't really want Lea in her home anyway. (Later on, Kelsey went so far as to become a foster parent to Lea.) But Ms. Brown was watching Kelsey very closely (with the help of "spies") when she would arrive in the morning and leave at the end of the day. Ms. Brown started to give Kelsey warnings if Kelsey arrived a minute or two late to school or left early (which rarely happened.) Unbeknownst to Kelsey at the time – Ms. Brown had Kelsey under a microscope 24 hours/day and was documenting. One Monday, Kelsey went home for lunch (she lived close) to wash Lea's clothes because they literally reeked. Upon her return, Ms. Brown humiliated Kelsey in front of office staff, saying she was goofing off when she should be working. No matter what legitimate explanation Kelsey would give, Ms. Brown would not relent—ever. At the end of the school year, Ms. Brown told the district that Kelsey should be fired and included all the documentation which Kelsey did not know about. The documentation was basically mistruths. (Kelsey was in her first year in a new district and could be fired with no explanation.) Kelsey was told by the district to resign or get fired. Two new teachers at Kelsey's school were also told the same thing that June.

Kelsey was not about to resign. She went back to her teacher's union, and they told her what options she had. Kelsey was not going to send in her resignation—she was going to "grieve" it. She wanted to take this all the way, knowing that if she did not win – she might never be able to work as a counselor in a school district again. It took many months for Kelsey's case to be heard, and her union supported her all the way. In the end, she lost her case, and Kelsey was devastated beyond words. She eventually opened her own private practice.

What Should Have Happened? To have an effective relationship between a school counselor and the principal – there must be trust, respect, and communication. This clearly was not established on day one. Kelsey was just placed, and Ms. Brown did not attempt to get to know Kelsey. Kelsey had the role of counselor, and Ms. Brown did not allow Kelsey to carry out that role without inappropriate interference. Ms. Brown lacked professional skills and effective, ethical communication with staff. If school districts truly want their schools to be successful– they need to believe that the principal and counselor's relationship is instrumental in student success! The school district failed in doing its job of investigating Ms. Brown's ill-willed practices. When counselors last only one year at a certain school – there must be a reason why. The district did assign a principal mentor for one year with Ms. Brown, but that was it. That was after Kelsey was fired.

A counselor and principal need to be partners. They need to understand each other, trust each other, and be able to communicate to benefit not only the students, but also other staff members as well. The academic achievement of students will soar when this partnership is effective, and teachers will see their school in a positive climate with their own student successes!

whwhwhwhwhwhwhwhwhwhwhwhwhwhwhwhwhwhwhwhwhwh

Teachers may have the most important role in carrying out the restructuring plan. Teachers are instrumental in implementing changes in scheduling and making adjustments to various time frames. In schools where teachers are included in the initial stages of planning, many assist with research and participate in planning prior to the inception of plans which require change on their part. Teachers' support of innovation often increases the chance for success. Having teachers as part of the decision-making process may enhance the restructuring effort. On the other hand, Yukl (1994) made some interesting observations about group leadership. He stated that optimistic assumptions about group members' emotional stability and maturity might not be wise. Group-centered leadership, on the surface, may seem attractive, but democracy in the workplace may be idealistic and not realistic. Yukl explained that groups might not receive authority to carry out decisions, and others affected may not cooperate with the directives. Lack of regular communication, or isolation, may contribute to this problem. Yukl's comments suggest that group decision-making is not always the best solution in every case. Effective leadership that entrusts decision-making to teaching staff may need to prepare the staff members for their roles as decision-makers before turning over the authority to make restructuring decisions. Teachers who have been isolated may not be ready to work as part of teams invoking change in the school structure.

High school teachers tend to be isolated from one another simply by the structure of buildings and schedules. Bells send groups of students to various rooms, and usually, one teacher spends the school day with as many as six or seven groups, with 25 to 35 students in each group. Teachers use planning periods to run off tests, prepare assignments, grade papers, or line up equipment for use in their classes. Scheduled time for teachers to communicate with one another, according to Glickman (1993), is almost nonexistent. Glickman stated, "Most educators do not discuss teaching practices with one another except in contrived situations. Such matters rarely form the content of faculty meetings, teachers' lounge, hallway conversations, or telephone calls" (p. 20). A possible conclusion, then, is that teachers and administrators have limited time to collaborate and build trust among themselves, groups, and committees.

School buildings are seldom designed to provide places to combine classes on a regular basis. Glickman (1993) explained that if someone wanted to build a building that would keep people from communicating with others and promote individual and uncoordinated activities, that building would resemble an ordinary school. Some school buildings have the capacity to move walls for larger groups but may have impediments (bookshelves, wall fixtures, etc.) preventing movement, which could open the walls to other teachers and classes. Many high school teachers experience isolation from other colleagues most of each school day and throughout the school year. The building structure contributes to that seclusion. Berry (1995) contended that teachers need to become de-isolated from one another. Teachers not used to working as a team will often find change in the school structure more difficult to develop and implement because of their own lack of cooperation with other teachers.

Fullan (1991) and Fullan and Miles (1992) stated that obstacles to change, in addition to isolation, include lack of time for planning and preparing, and lack of time and opportunity to communicate with colleagues or to learn new ways of teaching. Time equates to money for school districts in order to provide teachers with the time away from students to learn and grow and analyze ways to restructure their schools and teaching methods. Senge (1990) determined that those policymakers of learning organizations who sincerely want change must make it possible for their members to create a new and improved learning organization. Senge (1990) stated: "At the heart of a learning organization is a shift of mind—from seeing ourselves as separate from the world to connected to the world—from seeing our problems caused by someone or something 'out there' to seeing how our own actions create the problems we experience. A learning organization is a place where people are continually discovering how they create their reality. And how they change it." (pp. 12-13)

When teachers believe that they make positive changes in their classrooms and their school systems and that they may improve the chances of success for their students, they may view the restructuring as a positive professional experience. This experience may include themselves, their students, and their school system. Johnson (1990) indicated that top-down directives seldom provide that realization. According to Goodlad (1984), a school that plans to improve "will improve slowly, if at all, if reforms are thrust upon them [teachers]" (p. 318). Johnson stated that teachers must "venture beyond their classrooms, fashioning new working relationships with their peers, and participating in decisions about their schools. As a group, they must become accountable for teaching standards and professional performance" (p. 341).

Hall and Hord (1987) discussed the importance of getting to the heart of the emotions of how teachers feel about the change process. In describing how teachers are reacting to change, Hall and Hard stated that "the emphasis is on what teachers are doing relative to a particular innovation . . . affect, perception, and feelings are left out" (p. 81). Once a change process has begun, teachers' energies are often drained. In addition to having approximately 150 to 180 students in classes such as math, English, science, or social studies, teachers have record keeping, lesson planning, paper grading, and other monitoring duties. Hall and Hord noted that restructuring involves additional committees, meetings, and input opportunities after school and in the evening beyond the school day, which add to teachers' duties. Adams and Salvaterra (1997) noted that when teachers move to a block schedule, they need to change "how instruction is delivered and what concepts will be developed. Because this task at first appears formidable, teacher anxiety begins in the first stages of implementation" (p. 52). In addition to curriculum adjustment, changing teaching delivery systems, participating on committees, attending meetings, and other obligations the restructuring requires, many teachers in high school are involved in activities as advisors and coaches, which also take time outside the school day. The extra time and effort restructuring planning takes may be large, and as a result, some teachers may be hesitant to participate in planning for change.

Lieberman and Miller (1990) explained that the emotions teachers experience vary but generally include anger, frustration, exhaustion, worry, skepticism, futility, discontentment, and/or fear. When design features include ways to help teachers establish a schedule comparable with professional considerations within which to work, the teachers' interest tends to increase in working for change. School restructuring planning occurs for many schools while teachers and administrators are in the process of performing full-time duties. Lieberman and Miller indicated that restructuring might require adjusting the full-time responsibilities of teachers and administrators to provide the time to plan.

The administrative approach to change may have a major impact on how teachers participate in, accept, and adjust to changes. Trust may be an essential ingredient for successful restructuring efforts. According to Gardner (1990), "There is much to be gained in winning the trust of constituents. A leader capable of inspiring trust is especially valuable in bringing about a collaboration among mutually conspicuous elements in a constituency" (p. 33). When principals and teachers can work as team members, their energies will be directed toward a common goal. Wolfe (1993) stated, "Extraordinary accomplishments [can be] made when [they] stop trying to dominate each other and try to find a solution together" (p. 25). Patterson, Purkey, and Parker (1986) remarked that the principal "also influences the culture of the school district by serving in the role of teacher. The effective leader continuously teaches the vision, values, mission, goals, and objectives of the organization to others" (p. 87). The principal, then, who demonstrates that he or she values the teachers and their roles in restructuring as part of the district's mission, has the potential to build trust among the teachers and themselves in the change process.

Teachers and administrators who form excellent and trusting working relationships and who have a plan they want to apply to their schools may find it advisable to include the policymakers early in the change process. Majchrzak (1984) stressed the need for clear, timely communication with the policymakers, as well as stakeholders, from the beginning and throughout the process of policy development and change. All the work, effort, research, and leadership of other groups may fail if the policymakers are not an integral part of the program from the beginning. Maintaining accreditations and fulfilling all state standards is often a primary concern for school boards. Majchrzak discussed the importance of preparing school board directors for potential conflict that change may create within the district and within the community. As teachers discuss changes, people around them often become aware of the teachers' concerns. Bass (1990) made it clear that board members do not like to be asked questions concerning major changes about which they are unaware. An open system, according to Bass, where all stakeholders are involved in researching, planning, and developing the program, will create an environment where trust builds, and participants experience ownership in the plans.

Summary

The literature review has included four main areas: effects on individuals of change in the workplace; change as a reform and a restructuring process in high schools; block scheduling as a form of change; and teachers' professional and personal involvement in change and restructuring. Throughout the nation, reform and restructuring in education are happening, and President Clinton's 1997 State of the Union speech called attention to the need to support and improve public education. Block scheduling is a form of restructuring that provides schools with a way to use time more in keeping with their reform goals. Kadel (1994) has indicated that America, in using the traditional agrarian-based calendar with the factory model seven-period or eight-period day, may be able to find more effective time frames for education. Blocks of time in various arrangements may open opportunities for the delivery of information to students that may presently be limited in the traditional schedule.

Although all stakeholders are important in making change, teachers may be the essential ingredient of any change process. When teachers are involved in the change process as partners whose ideas are valued, the process of restructuring has much more opportunity to succeed (Fullan, 1991; Hargreaves, 1994). Involving teachers is important, and research (Darrington, 1988) shows that teachers who embrace a change have a better chance of bringing about change. Change for teachers, however, is not a simple matter. Restructuring takes much more than a commitment to change. For teachers, many needs are involved and may need to be met for change to occur effectively.

Hord et al. (1987), through their Concerns-Based Adoption Model (CRAM), described change as a process, not an event, and they developed five additional phases in their model. Change, according to Hord et al., is personal, requires developmental growth, and needs to be explained concretely and clearly. For teachers to move to a block schedule as one means of restructuring, the following areas may be helpful: training, input from the outset of the restructuring concept for the school, partnership relationships with administrators, empowerment to make decisions, permission to fail, permission to grieve the loss of the familiar processes, and encouragement to try again (Fullan, 1991). Studies of various types of change, restructuring, and the success or failure of change may help educators currently involved in change. Research is lacking, however, in examining how teachers personally and professionally feel about the process they go through, igniting up their old ways of functioning for many years. Teachers, as they move away from familiar practice and toward new practice, find themselves, according to Bridges (1991) and Fullan (1991), confused about what they are giving up in order to accept a new way of operating. Studies that examine individual school districts and the teachers who have been part of the restructuring process may help teachers and administrators prepare more fully for change. In examining the depth of loss and the pain that change can bring to a professional educator, other educators may gain a richer understanding of experiences they may face or have already faced.

When I experienced as principal the planning and the implementation of the block schedule over a four-year period in a small high school, I personally and professionally changed my own belief system. The personal level of adjustment of the professional educator in making this magnitude of change has not been addressed enough in research. This study explores the personal and professional impact of change, or the transition from the familiar to the unfamiliar, on teachers who have experienced moving to the block schedule. I believe their experiences, as well as my own in this area, have farther reaching implications in regard to change than strictly in changing to block scheduling. This qualitative study includes elements of heuristic inquiry and as such, concentrates on the impact of the transition to block scheduling, leaving the reader to make any personal comparisons to change in general.

What Happened?

Johnny and the YMCA

Mary, Johnny's mom, was in a conference with the principal. Mary was explaining to her why Johnny should not have missed the field trip or have been sent home from school, why he should not have been punished for his "unsafe behavior" as he ran to catch up with a classmate he wanted to walk with—and stepped out of the crosswalk. The principal said that he also spat on the YMCA floor and threw a ball at a teacher. Mary suggested the teacher make a safety plan with Johnny before the next YMCA visit, including Johnny in the planning, so he could learn safety in a positive way—not deny him school attendance for two days—and the loss of a field trip on one of those days. Johnny has ASD, ADHD, and other 'labels' in his IEP.

During the conference, the principal received a call that Johnny was not cooperating on the playground. Both Mary and the principal went to the playground. Johnny was near the rock wall entry, huddled near it when Mary arrived. The principal had to stop at her office briefly, so she was not there when Mary arrived. Johnny went to his mother immediately when he saw her. He appeared sad and frightened. During the following scene, Johnny remained quiet, scared, and wide-eyed.

Donald, the head teacher, began dramatically explaining to Mary loudly for all to hear that Johnny had been running all over the front area of the outside court and would not do what staff asked him to do—just kept running away from them. Donald's voice was angry as he stressed the following phrases: "Since we can't touch him…!" and "It's because of Johnny's behavior at the Y we aren't there for PE today!" and "Johnny spit on the floor!" "He threw a ball and hit a teacher!" and "We can't go to the Y because Johnny ruined it, and the Y won't stand for that behavior!" More students gathered as Donald said more, using blaming, angry words. Johnny moved close to his mom, full of fear and tearful. Donald became so upset that he turned away angrily from the group and stormed off, throwing up his hands—a very dramatic display of his disgust and anger—like—giving up, stomping off, done.

Joan, the assistant principal, stepped toward Johnny and Mary, and she continued the verbal confrontation—blaming Johnny for the Y not letting the Academy 7/8 grade class come for PE due to Johnny's behavior. She reiterated Donald's comments about Johnny spitting on the Y floor, hitting a teacher with a ball. She added that Johnny was unsafe in the crosswalk while going to the Y. When she finished speaking, Mary and Johnny walked into the school for Johnny to go to his next class. He begged his mom softly, "Please take me away from here, Mom. Please let's go home," and "They don't want me here" "Please let's go home." Because Mary didn't want him to leave school, she promised him that she would be in the hall area if he needed her. She told him kindly and softly, "I'll be checking in on you, Johnny. We need to work through this. You are strong, and you can do this." He went into class so sad, and Mary felt so very sad for him.

The Academy principal joined the group in process on the playground—late, but while she was there, she heard a portion of this scene with Donald and Joan dumping blame on Johnny, shaming him for his class not being able to go to the Y—his fault alone that the Y wouldn't let them all come to the Y for their class.

After Johnny went into his class, and because Mary felt so bad about this, she decided to go to the YMCA and apologize for Johnny's behavior. She wanted him to take responsibility for his actions, and she wanted to see just how bad he had been and how upset the Y was with him—denying the whole class from coming seemed like Johnny's behaviors must have been terrible.

At the YMCA Mary asked the girl at the desk if she was aware of the Academy classes not coming for their PE class that day. She said, "Let me get the Director." The Y director introduced herself. Mary asked about the Academy 7/8 class using the Y for PE. She said yes, happily. Mary began apologizing for Johnny's behavior. The Y director seemed puzzled. When Mary said that Johnny spat on the floor, the director laughed! "You can't imagine the mess people make here! I really know nothing about a student spitting on the floor, and no one would be denied coming to the Y for spitting on the floor." Mary told her that the teachers at Academy told her that the YMCA said they couldn't come today because of Johnny's behavior. The Y director said that Academy student groups have never been denied coming to the YMCA. Never. She said that the week before, she heard the teachers planning not to come this day, but Johnny was not even on her radar. She said that this was not the first time Academy staff had used the Y to deal with a student. She said that Academy students were great, that she enjoyed having them, and that she would never turn them away. She said she had 5 kids of her own—some with special needs, and she just felt the Academy kids needed and enjoyed being at the Y. She encouraged Mary to stand up for Johnny. She gave Mary her card and said, "Have the principal call me if she has any concerns. Johnny deserves better than a bunch of lying teachers blaming him for their decision."

When Mary returned to the Academy that same day, she told the principal about her visit. The director asked Mary for the Y director's card, and Mary gave it to her. She asked Mary to calm down—she was upset, said that Donald and Joan, both people she respected, had been involved in this lie and that they were so unprofessional to Johnny and to her as well since they knew she was listening to them along with many students. The principal asked Mary not to tell Johnny about this. She said that he was having a good day since the playground incident, and there was no need to upset him. "He really doesn't need to know any of this," "Telling him would just upset him," and "Think about Johnny and let's not let him know about this."

Mary told the principal that she was not going to let Johnny think that he was responsible for the class losing the Y for PE class. Mary told her that the teachers need to figure out a way to lift this blame from Johnny, help Johnny, and make sure all the other students realize that Johnny did not cause this loss—and that the teachers lied about it. Both Donald and Joan bullied, shamed, and embarrassed Johnny in front of his classmates and other students. Johnny deserves much better. The principal said, "Don't say anything right now. I'm meeting with the 7/8 staff after school about our previous meeting, and I'll deal with this, too."

At about 3:05, a staff member came out of the class and told Mary that Johnny was having problems and that she should take him home. Mary went to the class and looked in to see Johnny at his desk and three teachers sort of circling him, standing around him at a distance of a desk between them and Johnny. If Mary were Johnny, she thought, she would feel very intimidated. Three adults loomed over him, moving toward him or standing near him. Other adults and the students were watching this scene, especially watching Johnny. Mary entered the room and asked Johnny to come with her. One of the staff asked to talk with Mary. Mary reminded Johnny to bring his backpack, and she walked out with the staff person. She explained that Johnny was getting upset, and she wanted Mary to come into the room and see how he was acting and to help settle him down. Johnny joined them in the stair area. Mary told her that she appreciated that. The teacher then went into Johnny's behavior at the YMCA and how the Y wouldn't let the class come. Quietly, out of Johnny's hearing, Mary turned away from Johnny and softly said to her, "The story about Johnny causing the Y to refuse Academy students stops right now. It is not true. The principal will be talking with staff after school, but no more lies—the Y did not refuse Academy students because of Johnny. No more lies." Mary thanked her for her kindness toward Johnny at other times and that she appreciated her being caring toward him. Johnny and Mary left for home. A shocked teacher watched Mary and Johnny walk away.

On the way out the door, Johnny asked, "Am I in trouble?"

Mary told him, "Not with me, and I'll bet things are better tomorrow. Let's go home!" Mary gave him a reassuring hug—he actually let her hug him—and they went to the car.

Interestingly enough—Johnny picked out two trays of cookies when we stopped at the store to give his class the next day. Mary brought them in from the car and gave them to Johnny at the classroom door, but Johnny stopped. He didn't want to go into the room. "Please, mom, don't make me go into the room. They don't like me."

Mary took the cookies to the door, and a staff person took them into the room. "From Johnny," Mary said to the teacher.

The teacher stepped out and welcomed Johnny to class. "I'm so glad to see you, Johnny," The teacher smiled and brought him into the classroom.

What could have happened? The entire staff could have conducted themselves professionally. They did not. Their treatment of Johnny was despicable. The principal's attempts to cover up the teachers' scheme were also despicable and unprofessional.

What did happen? They demoralized a student in front of many other students, using humiliation to control him. They loudly and dramatically demonstrated anger to sell their lies to all of the students, and they dramatically bullied Johnny several times over a fabricated incident. They also lied to the student's parent. Johnny was traumatized and did not want to ever go back to school. Johnny had nightmares and constant fear of attending school for quite a while. His mother attended school each day, staying in the hall, so Johny could check to see that she was there. The parents did not continue Johnny's enrollment there for the next school year.

The two teachers most responsible for the unprofessional conduct toward Johnny did not want to own up to their behavior, but the next day, Mary brought Johnny to each of them and said that the teachers wanted to apologize to him for blaming him for the class not getting to go to the YMCA. Mary also went into the classroom while both teachers explained to the class members that they were "mistaken" about Johnny, causing them not to be able to go to the YMCA. Mary spoke up, "The teachers had decided the week before that they were not going to the YMCA the day you thought you missed. Right?" Both teachers admitted that was true. They then each said to Johnny, "We're sorry, Johnny."

As Mary left the classroom, she whispered to Johnny that she would be in the hallway anytime he needed her and that the Y situation was not his fault.

Johnny said, "Good! That's over!" Many weeks later, Johnny finally slept through the night.

Unprofessional behavior should never be tolerated. Parents have an obligation to support their children. The depression, sadness, fear, and anxiety that this type of incident can create for children is unacceptable. The best time to deal with these issues is immediately while people remember the details and before the student has too many sleepless nights and fearful school days, building up sadness and anxiety.

How does this relate to schedule changes? Unfortunately, some teachers may lie about their involvement to protect their own interests. A few Academy teachers used intimidation and fear to make Johnny frightened into obedience. The major changes required to move to a major schedule change can drive some participants to drastic measures. Planning together, protecting one another, and bringing outliers into the group in honest, professional, and kind ways may save the whole project from failure. One "bad apple" can ruin the whole basket.

whwhwhwhwhwhwhwhwhwhwhwhwhwhwhwhwhwhwhwhwhwhwh

CHAPTER III: RESEARCH METHODOLOGY

Qualitative Research and Heuristic Inquiry

This chapter presents the specific category of the chosen methodology and why the chosen methodology meets the needs of this study. The chapter also includes the design of the study, how this form applies to this research, implementation of the study, researcher roles, and the limitations of the study.

Qualitative Research

The general method of research this study follows is qualitative research. Although both quantitative and qualitative research methods are used in educational studies, certain advantages accompany this type of study that contributed to my choice of methodology. According to Patton (1990), qualitative methods have an openness, unconstrained by predetermined categories of analyses, unlike quantitative methods. In quantitative research, standardized measures often establish limits confined to predetermined response categories. Patton explained that the researcher has assigned numbers to responses to attain data from large samples of populations. An advantage of quantitative analysis is a large number of people from whom the information can be gathered, analyzed, and then generalized to a broad population. The quantitative evaluation tool, such as a test or a survey, however, is not usually administered personally, and other considerations of a unique nature are not described. Often thousands of people participate in quantitative research, and the product can be useful for understanding the broad scope of the research topic. Qualitative methods, in contrast, provide in-depth information rich with descriptions about a small number of people, and as Wertz (1987) indicated, qualitative research finds the researcher trying to make sense of what he or she observed or received directly from participants. To analyze elements of meaning, interior thoughts and reactions, and feelings and fears, the qualitative researcher extends deeper into a limited field on a personal level.

Gherardi and Turner (1987) explained that the researcher needs to know when the nature of the research requires numbers, when the research data are non-standardized, and when counting would be inappropriate. Indications that guide the researcher in the choice of paradigms, according to Cook and Reichardt

(1979), include characteristics of both quantitative and qualitative research. For example, quantitative research includes obtrusive and controlled measurement, generates replicable data, and is generalizable, particularistic, and outcome-oriented. Qualitative research, however, is naturalistic and uncontrolled observation, which results in rich, deep, or real data and is not generalized to a larger population (Patton, 1982; Tesch, 1990). Qualitative research often involves single case studies which are holistic and process-oriented. Because each of these methods views the world in different ways, a researcher, according to Patton (1982), may decide on the method that will provide the information on the level the researcher desires (Cook and Reichardt, 1979). In this project, I hope to provide rich data about one high school and a select few teachers and administrators who have in-depth experiences to share. The qualitative method most clearly reflects the purpose of this inquiry.

This qualitative endeavor meets several criteria. Unlike quantitative studies, which deal with "what" and "how many," this study answers the questions "why" and "how," the focus involves a particular phenomenon. It is descriptive; it involves being in the field with the subjects of the research (Merriam, 1958; Brewer and Collins, 1981). According to Patton (1986): "Quantitative measures are succinct, parsimonious, and easily aggregated for analysis; they are systematic, standardized, and easily presented in a short space. By contrast, qualitative responses are longer, more detailed, and variable in content; analysis is difficult because responses are neither systematic nor standardized" (p. 11).

Heuristic Inquiry

A further definitive characteristic of this study is also defined, according to Patton (1990), as having elements of heuristic inquiry. Patton stated, "Heuristic inquiry asks: What is my experience of this phenomenon and the essential experience of others who also experience this phenomenon intensely? The researcher must have personal experience with and an intense interest in the phenomenon under study" (p. 71). I have experienced as a principal the intense response created by moving from a traditional schedule to a block schedule. I am aware of the trauma this change created for some teachers on my staff. My own involvement and interest in how change affected my staff and me during a four-year period in a public high school are the reasons that I have become committed to researching this phenomenon.

Douglas and Moustakas (1984) stated, "Heuristics is concerned with meanings, not measurements; with essence, not appearance; with quality, not quantity; with experience, not behavior (p. 42). Douglas and Moustakas described the heuristic inquiry as seeing subjects open to succumbing or yielding to the subject of the research, a giving up of personal control "to be tumbled about with the newness and drama of a search focus that is taking over life" (p. 47). Patton (1990) stated that because the researcher has been part of similar changes, the researcher and the participants necessarily become connected as they examine together the nature of this human experience. Patton explained the meaning and significance this change conveys to the participants, and the researcher brings them together as they examine their feelings through the research process.

Heuristic research requires observations, dialogues with those involved in the process (including oneself), and in-depth interviews. Craig (1978) stated, "[Heuristic inquiry] affirms the possibility that one can live deeply and passionately in the moment, be fully immersed in the mysteries and the miracles, and still be engaged in meaningful research" (p. 20). Douglas and Moustakas (1984) described heuristic inquiry's strength as follows: "The power of heuristic inquiry lies in its potential for disclosing the truth. Through exhaustive self-research, dialogues with others, and creative depictions of experience, comprehensive knowledge is generated, beginning as a series of subjective understandings and developing into a systematic and definitive exposition" (p. 40).

Moustakas (1994) outlined six phases of heuristic research as "the initial engagement, immersion into the topic and question, incubation, illumination, explication, and the culmination of the research in a creative synthesis" (p. 18). Moustakas stressed the importance of returning to the research participants often, sharing with them their transcriptions for further analysis, and ensuring that participants have given information accurately, reflecting their feelings, attitudes, and truths in regard to the experience. The focus of heuristic inquiry, according to Moustakas, is "exclusively and continually aimed at understanding human experience" (p. 19).

I have included elements of heuristic inquiry in this qualitative case study because of my personal experience and closeness to the subject. Patton (1990) warned that closeness to the subject could compromise objective reporting of the data. Patton stated, "[In heuristic inquiry] the researcher is the primary instrument . . . that challenges in the extreme traditional scientific concerns about researcher objectivity and detachment" (p. 73). Through many visitations, incubation of the material after collection, and immersion in the research data over time, I strived to reach the reality of this experience for those who participated, as well as for myself (Craig, 1978; Moustakas, 1994).

Heuristic inquiry has both common and differing characteristics from other types of qualitative research. Moustakas (1994) and Patton (1990) both indicated that ethnography focuses on the culture of a group of people requiring intensive fieldwork. The ethnographic researcher becomes immersed in the culture by participating in direct observations of activities of the culture over an extended period of time. Heuristic research focuses on discovering the nature and meaning of experiences. The researcher becomes immersed in the study and, through visitations, observations, dialogues, and interviews, discovers the depth of the experience. The researcher has also shared similar experiences in a different setting (Moustakas, 1994).

Grounded theory research, according to Glaser and Straus (1967), develops a theory based on the initial phases of research which seeks to define an experience. The researcher then works toward finding an explanation of the nature and the meaning of the experience as it relates to a particular group of people. The researcher does not share a similar experience as in heuristic inquiry, and the grounded theory researcher constantly seeks to fill gaps in the information through interviews, not through observations. Observations are an essential part of heuristic research (Moustakas, 1994).

Phenomenology seeks the structure and essence of the experience of a specific phenomenon for a particular group of people. Patton (1990) stated, "The phenomenon experienced may be an emotion—loneliness, jealousy, anger. The phenomenon may be a program, an organization, or a culture" (p. 69). Heuristic inquiry focuses on an experience shared by the researcher with the people who are participants in the study. Phenomenology, according to Husseri (1962), was "The study of how people describe things and experience them through their senses" (p. 69).

"Hermeneutic research asks," according to Patton (1990), "What are the conditions under which a human act took place, or a product was produced that makes it possible to interpret its meanings" (p. 84)? In heuristic inquiry, the researcher is known and part of the study. The heuristic research concentrates on the experience rather than the interpretation of the experience.

After considering the various types of research available, I have incorporated elements of heuristic inquiry in the qualitative study (Patton, 1990). I have had experience with block scheduling development and transition, and I bring personal insights into the research process. Additionally, the setting is a public high school, and the circumstances of restructuring through block scheduling are similar to my experiences. I believe I can share both my experiences and the experiences of the educators selected for this inquiry. The resulting information may benefit other educators in Washington and/or other states. This study may be helpful to educators and their communities who are considering or who are already in the process of restructuring to a block schedule.

Many schools in Washington, as well as in many other states, have selected a variety of forms of block scheduling as part of restructuring plans. Because school personnel are involved in teaching, which usually takes a full commitment of professional time, changes in schedule may not be analyzed in an in-depth manner. However, the results may have a strong impact on teachers and others involved in the change process. This research may provide another view of understanding to teachers and administrators considering block scheduling. The teachers of the school, which is the subject of my research, have shared experiences that may help other school faculties understand their own experiences. This information may make the transition more comprehensible, if not easier, for other educators in the process of restructuring. According to Stake (1995), the purpose of qualitative research is to understand more fully the human experience. By adding to the body of knowledge in the area of restructuring and how specific teachers have responded to this change in their professional and personal lives, this study may enrich the information available to school personnel who are considering similar changes.

Implementation and Design of the Study

This section explains how the study and the steps required for the process to take place. The design of the study includes a description of the collection of data through the interview process, dialogues, and site visitations, followed by an explanation of processing the data by means of a coding system.

Implementation

Implementation of this study involved several steps. I obtained initial permission and final authorization to do the study, completed the consent procedure, made site visitations and observations, selected participants for dialogues, initiated the dialogues, and conducted two interviews with administrators.

Obtaining Initial and Official Permission

During the 1996-1997 school year, Shadle Park High School, which I chose to study, implemented a block schedule. I visited the school and discussed my interest in research involving block scheduling with the principal, who encouraged me to make visitations as I had time. The principal invited me to attend specific meetings and programs, including four teacher training sessions and departmental meetings. I also made visitations at times of my own choosing throughout the school year. Each time I made a visitation, I called in advance to let the principal and any individual teacher affected by my visit know I would be coming, and I checked in at the office upon arrival prior to any observations, dialogues, or conferences with teachers in regard to dialogues.

In March 1996, I applied for permission to undertake the research at Shadle Park High School from the Spokane School District's Research Committee. This committee screens all research projects conducted in the district's schools and other facilities. Its screening procedure includes an application process and an interview with the researcher and the committee. I met the committee on April 17, 1997. Four members of the committee interviewed me, and one week later, I was notified that the district's board of directors had approved my application. I was able to begin immediately conducting my research at my chosen site.

The Design of the Study

The design of this qualitative inquiry has two important goals. The first goal is to determine what made it possible for the teachers to change in the restructuring process of moving from a traditional schedule to a block schedule. As part of this goal, I dialogued with teachers to determine what may have facilitated for them the ability to make the transition from the traditional schedule to the block schedule. The second goal is to examine the impact both professionally and personally that this change has had on the teachers who participated in this study. I made site visitations, conducted dialogues with ten teachers, and interviewed two administrators who were actively involved in planning and implementing the block schedule.

Heuristic inquiry enhances qualitative techniques, according to Moustakas (1994). The holistic description of qualitative research could generate insights into the experiences teachers encounter through dialogues with me that quantitative techniques do not reach. Moustakas formulated a formal, 5-phase approach to heuristic inquiry. The first phase, "immersion," requires full involvement from the researcher. The researcher lives and breathes the experience, letting all of his or her senses become acute to the site, people, and all other characteristics related to the study. The second phase is "incubation." The researcher allows time for the total experience to become part of his or her inner awareness, withdrawing to contemplate the meaning of the immersion event. "Illumination" is the third phase as the researcher encourages the immersion experience to take on deeper clarity and form patterns or groupings of information. The "explication" phase involves making connections and discovering relationships among patterns, focusing and further defining the experience. The fifth phase, "creative synthesis," is like a puzzle put together—all of the aspects of the experience become a creatively expressed, richly shared, and personally communicated analysis.

I did not follow these steps for heuristic inquiry formally, but rather, informally, because although I was directly involved as a participant in changing to a block schedule in Kettle Falls, I was not involved in this research at Shadle Park High School at that time. A year after leaving the principal position, my research was underway at Shadle Park High School, and as the qualitative study unfolded, I was aware of the strong recollection of my four-year position as principal and building leader at Kettle Falls High School as we planned and implemented the change to the block schedule. Because my empathy was acute as I became involved with the Shadle Park High School staff, I felt compelled to share, at least in an informal way, heuristic elements of my experience. Moustakas indicated that holistic experiences which heuristic inquiry provides might offer greater depth to research. Patton (1990) stated:

The holistic approach assumes that the whole is understood as a complex system that is greater than the sum of its parts; it also assumes that a description and understanding of a person's social environment or an organization's political context is essential to an understanding of what is observed. . . . it is insufficient simply to study and measure the parts of a situation by gathering data about isolated variables, scales, and dimensions. (pp. 49-50)

Patton noted that qualitative methods give researchers the ability to document differences and unusual or unique circumstances. People seeking individual and personal views from firsthand accounts of feelings, experiences, and/or emotional responses will find information of that nature in the heuristic elements of this research.

The Specific Format of the Study Includes the Following Steps:

1. I made frequent visits to Shadle Park High School throughout the 1996-97 school year. The purpose was to become acquainted with faculty and administrators to let them know that I would be researching block scheduling and to lay a foundation for building trust between them and me.

2. I requested permission to research from the school district of the high school where I planned to research. Once I had been granted official permission, I began dialogues and interviews, as indicated in items 3 and 4.

3. I initiated and participated in dialogues with ten teachers. By direction of the principal, every teacher on staff received an invitation in his or her school mailbox to discuss block scheduling with me. The purpose of this note was to eliminate the feeling that this project was limited to only certain teachers. In addition, the two administrators included in this study made recommendations to me of teachers I could seek out for dialogue purposes. In granting permission for the study, the Spokane School District Research Committee members indicated that the administrators could assist in recruiting teachers to participate. The two administrators recommended teachers with several levels of experience and with a variety of levels of involvement and success in the block scheduling process. Any teacher who chose to be involved would have been included, even if it meant increasing the number of participants in the study. Both Denzin (1970) and Patton (1990) stressed the importance of accuracy in recording data. To be sure I had recorded each teacher's information accurately, I shared individual dialogue notes with each participant. I made adjustments as each teacher indicated in order to have the completely correct information. In addition, I gave each teacher a copy of the correct dialogues. Dialogues will remain confidential between each teacher and me.

4. I interviewed two administrators. I taped these interviews and fully transcribed all information. I used an open questioning strategy to allow the administrator to build on a question as he or she deemed necessary. Tapes and transcripts are confidential. I gave each administrator a complete copy of the transcribed interview for review and corrections to ensure the information was correct.

5. Following interviews, I shared information with only the individual who
    gave me the information and kept all dialogues and interviews
    confidential. I explained to each person that nothing each one said would
    be identified with him or her personally. Patton (1990) reinforced the
    necessity of confidentiality between interviewer and interviewee. I
    adjusted information as directed by the two administrators after
    conferring with the individuals who gave me the information to be sure
    I had the content and the meaning of each dialogue or interview
    accurately recorded.

The Interview Process

I conducted two interviews, one each with two administrators. The
interviewees expressed a positive interest in participating, and we seemed to have
had a positive relationship. Communication seemed open and natural. Patton
(1990) commented on the importance of respecting the people being interviewed
and establishing rapport, as well as neutrality:

Rapport means that I respect the people being interviewed, so what they say
is important because of who is saying it. I want to convey to them that their
knowledge, experiences, attitudes, and feelings are important. Yet, I will not judge
them for the content of what they say to me. Rapport is built on the ability to
convey empathy and understanding without judgment (p. 317)

Each interviewee agreed to participate and signed a consent form. The
consent form provided subjects the option of discontinuing the research
participation at any time, an essential procedure. Babbie (1995) discussed the
importance of making sure participants are not harmed in any way through the
research process. A waiver was part of the consent form to limit the liability of
the researcher. Anonymity and confidentiality are also part of the consent form
and are the ethical responsibilities of the researcher to protect (Babbie, 1995). I
coded the names of participants and later removed names from any records. I
stored research records and information in a locked container in my home (Patton,
1990) following the completion of the research. After five years, I destroyed the
stored records and information.

The interview questions follow an interview guide approach. This approach,
according to Patton (1990): "Provides topics or subjects within which the
interviewer is free to explore, probe, and ask questions that will elucidate and
illuminate that particular subject. Thus the interviewer remains free to build

conversation within a particular subject area, to word questions spontaneously, and to establish a conversational style—but with the focus on a particular subject that has been determined" (p. 283).

This format may encourage the interviewer to respond using extended answers, exploring beyond what he or she has done as a response to change. Interviewees may see the topics and issues that are usually in outline form prior to the interview, and this may help the flow of conversation during the interview (Patton, 1990). Having interviewees share how they felt about the various aspects of change helped me learn what in the process worked well for them individually and for their colleagues. The guided questioning format was used consistently during the two administrators' interviews.

In following Patton's (1990) directions in the content of questions, I included the following types of questions: experience/behavior questions, opinion/value questions, feeling questions, knowledge questions, sensory questions, and background/demographic questions. Stake (1995) observed: "The qualitative interviewer should arrive with a short list of issue-oriented questions, possibly handing the respondent a copy . . . the purpose, for the most part, is not to get simple yes or no answers, but the description of an episode, a linkage, an explanation. Formulating questions and anticipating probes that evoke good responses is a special art" (p. 65).

Babbie (1965) suggested using frequent probes on initial responses to encourage additional information. I found this helpful in both interviews and dialogues, although I did not need to use probes often. I also found that the people I interviewed and with whom I dialogued were eager to participate in the interviews and dialogues and displayed genuine interest in sharing their experiences.

Observations and Visitations

I observed classes of the teachers with whom I dialogued, and I visited classrooms and teachers' meetings throughout the 1996-1997 school year. Each observation varied from 15 to 45 minutes, and the time involved in dialogues varied from 20 minutes to over an hour each time, depending on the availability of the teachers. I met with the teachers several times during the two-year period of data collection. The principal invited me to many meetings, and I requested to attend meetings dealing with block scheduling. These observations and visitations helped me become more familiar with teachers and helped them also become more familiar with me. As a result, the participants of both dialogues and interviews became known to me and I to them. My impression of our interactions was positive.

Patton (1986) described the various roles of a researcher as an observer, participant observer, observer as a participant, and interviewer. I was an observer at times in observing classes and some meetings. Occasionally, I was an observer as a participant when, at a few meetings, teachers or administrators asked me direct questions. Not responding to questions asked may have created an awkward and unnatural situation. Near the beginning of the school year, the principal introduced me as a visitor and researcher who had worked with block scheduling. I kept my responses to their questions brief and did not interject questions of my own. I did not take notes at meetings because I felt that note-taking might distract or inhibit others attending. While conducting dialogues with the ten teachers, I was a participant observer, actively involved in dialogues. Following each dialogue, I went to a quiet place and took notes as quickly as I could to retain the dialogue as closely as possible to its exact wording. I did not take notes during the dialogue because I felt it would interfere with the flow of the conversation. As an interviewer, I was also a participant observer, actively listening, using probes as needed, and contributing to the flow of information from the interviewees.

Processing the Data

I made every attempt to record information accurately without bias. Word processed transcriptions of interviews and dialogues include all responses in their entirety with the added review by each person with whom I dialogued and interviewed to eliminate error. Patton (1990) stated that data needed to be horizontalized, or treated as of equal importance, examined thoroughly, and organized into clusters. By coding various areas that occur in the interviews and dialogues, I watched for repetitious information, as well as extraneous and inconsequential data to eliminate. Denzin (1989) stated that the researcher needs to take apart and dissect all data by using the following steps:

1. Locate within the personal experience, or self-story, key phrases and statements that speak directly to the phenomenon in question.
2. Interpret the meanings of these phrases as an informed reader.
3. Obtain the subject's interpretations of these phrases, if possible.
4. Inspect these meanings for what they reveal about the essential, recurring features of the phenomenon being studied.

5. Offer a tentative statement, or definition, of the phenomenon in terms of the essential recurring features identified in step 4. (pp. 55-56)

Following these steps will help eliminate researcher bias from the data.

The Role of the Researcher

My most important duty is to demonstrate trustworthiness and dependability to the people involved in this research process. The interviews and dialogues may be hollow and meaningless if the persons interviewed do not feel they can trust me to present an accurate, sensitive picture of their feelings and their experiences. I have an ethical responsibility to make appropriate role choices. The following sections further develop the ethics and limitations of research.

whwhwhwhwhwhwhwhwhwhwhwhwhwhwhwhwhwhwhwhwhwhwhwhwhwhwh

What Happened?

Teacher Experiences Board Member Angst

What happens to ethical behavior when a person in power in a school district forces his or her way into the change process or any part of the operation of a school district?

A state awarded teacher considered outstanding in her field was targeted to be cut from her teaching position due to budget constraints. She had seniority, and the teachers union supported her case to the State Supreme Court, which found in her favor.

Background: This teacher had assigned her class (like she did every year) to write a research paper on an American literature topic. Students were required to organize their research notes on note cards (a graded activity) and then use their notes to assist them in writing the research paper. One student (a school board member's son) turned in acceptable notecards; however, he turned in a final product on a totally different subject for which he had no notecards. This teacher showed the notecards and the research paper to the principal, who agreed that the student had not done the assignment as given, the notecards and the final paper were not related in any way, and the final product did not appear to be the work of that student, rather it seemed like a paper written by a more experienced writer for a college class. Under school rules, the student should have failed the course for plagiarism—claiming work not his own and turning it in for a grade. However, this teacher told the student that she would not accept his research paper as it was given to her, that he needed to write the final paper on the same subject as his notecards expressed to receive credit. If he did not do this, he would fail for plagiarism. She told him that if he did his own work to the best of his ability, she would give him full credit for his work, even though he had tried to pass off this other paper as his own. The teacher felt parental pressure and participation may have played a major role in his turning in this paper that he did not write. The teacher preferred having the student write the research paper; failing was too much punishment for what another person may have encouraged–or forced him to do..

What else happened? This board member pushed the board to cut this teacher and replace her with a less experienced, less expensive teacher. He explained to the board that by cutting her position, her husband, also an experienced teacher, would probably also resign. They would move elsewhere, allowing the board to hire two less expensive teachers to replace her and her husband. The board member was bent on getting rid of the teacher who figured out that someone cheated (he or his wife). He did not think about how hard it would be to replace both teachers and the subjects they taught. He just wanted her to go far away from this community. She was the "evidence" of his cheating.

What could have happened? The teacher was heartbroken at first. Being cut from a long-term position is an emotional and personal loss. She could have given up, stayed in place, and just accepted this blow to her career, her family, and her personality.

Her husband could have stayed with the job. Moving their daughter, who was a sophomore in high school, was a major concern. Fortunately, their daughter wanted to move.

The board member, driven by anger, personal guilt, and a need for vengeance, could have stopped his vendetta against this teacher and encouraged his son to write the paper as all other students did to meet the class requirements for a better grade.

What did happen? The teacher's position was cut. The student did not make an effort to write the paper. The teacher, the next year, attended a university and earned a master's degree and a secondary principal certificate. The results of the State Supreme Court's decision came a year after she was cut, awarding reinstatement of her position and pay for the year she was cut. She chose not to return to her teaching position. She was hired as a principal in another school; her husband also was hired near her new school. They sold their home and moved to their new community. Their daughter began her junior year in a new school and graduated as valedictorian. She was a state-level athlete in three sports in her new school.

The board hired less experienced teachers to replace both teachers. The board member responsible for creating this incident had let his anger drive his actions. His "victory" hurt his school district and the students who could have had more qualified teachers for many years into the future.

How does this fit into the change process? Beware of the power-seekers who will force their will on others, regardless of what is good for the school district. If a board member, administrator, influential teacher, staff member, parent, or community member has control issues and is set against any aspect of the change process, that person(s) can create havoc anywhere along the change process, even bringing an excellent plan and process to a screeching halt.

whwhwhwhwhwhwhwhwhwhwhwhwhwhwhwhwhwhwhwhwhwh

Ethics

Stake (1995) pointed out that "the researcher, deliberately or intuitively, makes role choices . . . including:

- a. How much to participate personally in the activity of the case
- b. How much to pose as an expert, whether to be a neutral observer or evaluate as a critical analyst
- c. How much to try to serve the needs of anticipated readers
- d. How much to provide interpretations about the case
- e. How much to advocate a position
- f. Whether or not to tell it as a story

But perhaps the most important choice is how much will the researcher be her- or himself. (p. 103)

Patton (1990) indicated that the researcher's roles might vary with different people in different circumstances. The researcher is guided by an ethical responsibility, making honest choices and decisions throughout the process. By avoiding conscious bias, using techniques to test the data, and horizontalizing the data, the researcher can use a delimitation process to make sure the data is clean. Peshkin (1988) stated that researcher bias might be checked by "formal, systematic monitoring of self" (p. 20).

In conversations prior to interviews and dialogues, I assured participating teachers and administrators that the information they shared with me would be confidential between each individual and me. Patton (1990) expressed the need for the researcher to provide the following information prior to gathering interview and dialogue information: "What will be asked, who is the information for, how will the information be handled, including confidentiality, what is the purpose of collecting the information, and how will it be used" (p. 328).

Following dialogues and interviews, I provided teachers and administrators with complete transcripts for their review, corrections, and/or additions so the participants would feel confident about the accuracy of the information I was using about them. Shils (1959) noted the importance of full disclosure of information and invited the participant to review the transcriptions of their individual dialogues or interviews. I believe I provided an avenue of trust with each participant and that my intent with the resulting research was to do no harm to them or to the institution they represent.

Limitations

Being the person I am may be a limiting factor for the heuristic element of this study. Because I have experienced a similar phenomenon, I may inadvertently intrude upon or manipulate the study due to my personal reactions to information. According to Patton (1990), "For heuristic inquiry to occur, the researcher *must* have personal experience with the *intense interest* in the phenomena under study. Second, others who are part of the study must share an intensity of experience with the phenomenon" (p. 71). As a result, Patton noted that heuristic inquiry "challenges in the extreme traditional scientific concerns about researcher objectivity and detachments" (p. 73).

In coding information from individual participants, then bracketing experiences from individuals into topics, such as fear or frustration, I attempted to eliminate bias. Denzin (1989) explained bracketing as confronting subject matter on its own terms. Patton (1990) stated, "Once the data are bracketed, all aspects of the data are treated with equal value" (p. 408). This is a delimiting process that may keep the researcher from giving one person's experiences too much attention. By concentrating on the experience itself through the accounts of many participants, I hope I reduced the possibility of my own experiences dominating the interpretation of the experiences of the participants in this study.

The nature of qualitative research may bring concerns to readers since it is rich, in-depth research of relatively few subjects rather than qualitative research, which may involve information from thousands of participants. Patton (1990) noted that both fields have limitations, and both bring valuable information forward for review. This qualitative study with elements of heuristic inquiry may provide rich, in-depth research about one group of teachers and two administrators involved in change. The results may be helpful to others involved in change.

Analysis of Data

The analysis of data followed an inductive, thematic approach, which, according to Lincoln and Guba (1985), makes sense of data. Inductive data analysis seeks to find the information within and pull it forth to make it clear. Patterns found among the teachers, contrasting information developed, and information that does not make connections with what research has already discovered emerged. Inductive reasoning helped make connections where they existed and presented information as well.

I word-processed information from interviews and dialogues and, as Stake (1995) indicated, coded the information so that similar information may be assembled from them. This process, Lincoln and Guba (1985) noted, defines units and identifies them for further analysis. A segment of data can be categorized even if information is not in complete form. The segment of a sentence, a whole sentence, or a paragraph. From these segments, a researcher establishes topics and categories. I established the number of codes necessary as I analyzed the interviews and dialogues. Once I categorized and coded all of the data, I gave equal value to all aspects of the data by assembling together like-coded information from dialogues and interviews. Denzin (1989) referred to this process as horizontalizing the data. After spreading the information out and examining it as having equal value, I then organized the data into meaningful clusters. I included all dialogues and interviews, as well as observation information when I determined clusters of data.

As the only researcher gathering and analyzing data, I needed to do all I could to eliminate researcher bias in interpreting results. In this study, I have had a similar experience in which I was immersed for four years. In this research experience, I chose to use an urban school since the school of my experience was a rural school. To help me view the research objectively, I chose this urban school because it was applying a block schedule different from the one I had helped develop and implement. I used horizontalizing techniques (Denzin, 1989) to correct for bias and filter out bias to the best of my ability. Because the purpose of my research was to share the experiences of teachers and administrators in one urban high school as these people acted, reacted, and emotionally responded to the change process, I needed to refrain from making judgments about the process, the individuals involved, their experiences, and the application of block schedules.

To gain from administrators the most thorough information I could in the interview process, I chose to use the guided question interview process. Guided questioning strategies have limitations. According to Patton (1990), "Important and salient topics may be inadvertently omitted. Interviewer flexibility in sequencing and wording questions can result in substantially different responses from different perspectives, thus reducing the comparability of responses" (p. 288). I was strongly aware of the negative possibilities of using this format for questioning to avoid the possible negative consequences of this form of questioning.

The limited number of people being interviewed and with whom I dialogued did not provide as much information as would be provided if I interviewed and dialogued with many teachers and administrators. I believe that the teachers who volunteered to participate and whom the administrators recommended provided the quality of information necessary for reasonable results. Administrators made recommendations based on having worked as colleagues with the teachers for at least five years. Their knowledge of these teachers exceeded mine as a researcher, and I believe the cross-section of teaching areas and experiences the recommended teachers represented enriched the study. The administrators may have biases in their recommendations which could have emerged and affected the quality of the research. Having the administrators make recommendations was the preferred method of selecting teachers by the Spokane School District Research Committee due to the knowledge base of the people within the school and staff as compared to the limited knowledge base of a visiting researcher. The two administrators in this study supported my including any other teachers or administrators as participants in the study, regardless of administrator recommendation. Two of the ten teachers involved in dialogues were not among those chosen by administrators.

Selected teachers could choose, at any time, to discontinue the process. Replacing the person or persons or eliminating a person's information near the end of the study could affect the quality of the study. Information gathered near the beginning of the study could lose impact compared to information gathered toward the end of the study. The people involved may have adjusted to change and may have forgotten the intensity of the initial experiences when they were involved in dialogues during the second year. Current information and experiences may have the predominant part of the memory of any of the interviewees and dialogue participants. For example, a teacher involved in a summer training session may remember most of the information he or she experienced during the training. Patton (1990), regarding limitations of qualitative research, stated, *"The principal is to report any personal and professional information that may have affected data collection, analysis, and interpretation [italics in original]*—either negatively or positively—in the minds of users of the findings" (p. 472).

Summary

This chapter presented a contrast between qualitative and quantitative research methodology with reasons given for the selection of qualitative research for this study. The qualitative inquiry that reflects the case study method, including elements of heuristic inquiry, is the specific type of research I selected due to my personal and professional experience with the topic of the research. The design of the research and its implementation were presented, along with a description of the steps I followed in carrying out the research study. I have reviewed the role of the researcher and the importance of accurate, ethical preparation and evaluation of information. I explained the limitations of the study and, as a researcher, my obligation to eliminate bias from the research in recording and evaluating information. This is essential to the value of the study.

CHAPTER IV: DATA

The Role of the Administrator in Facilitating Change and the Components of the Change Process

This chapter presents the research from two years of site visits, several dialogues with ten teachers, and interviews with two administrators. These educators have shared their personal and professional experiences in the change process as they moved from a traditional seven-period school day to a unique block schedule which they call a modified AB block schedule. This schedule, on Mondays, had six periods of 50-minute duration. On Tuesdays and Thursdays, the first three periods met for 100 minutes each. On Wednesdays and Fridays, the last three periods met for 100 minutes each. Teachers had a 50-minute preparation period on Mondays. During the remaining four days each week, teachers were scheduled for two 100-minute preparation periods (one every other day).

Information in this chapter explains the initial stages of changing to a block schedule, the time frame in which the change to the block schedule occurred, and the implementation of the new block schedule. Some of the participants in the study were involved in leadership roles from the initial planning stages, some became involved as the process developed, and some were not involved at all in planning or designing the schedule. This chapter describes the various levels of involvement of ten teachers and two administrators and their professional and personal reactions to the change process. Pseudonyms are used for the ten teachers and the two administrators to provide anonymity for participants. Other individuals quoted who were not interviewed are not named but referred to according to their job classification of "teacher" or "administrator."

The educators involved in this study experienced the change process in different ways. Their individual change experiences included a wide range of emotional responses on both professional and personal levels. Changes in teaching styles, methods, and/or materials were potential concerns for some participants in making this adjustment to a new time frame for teaching. This chapter describes the emotional characteristics these educators experienced, as well as accommodations in the previous teaching methods they chose to make as they changed to a block schedule. The roles of administrators in implementing change, working with teachers in the change process, and the administrators' assistance—or lack of assistance—in helping teachers adjust to change are also a focus of this chapter. Because this research has elements of heuristic inquiry, I interject my own experiences that relate to similar changes from being involved in moving from a traditional schedule to a block schedule in another school district.

The first area of consideration in this chapter deals with the initial stages of changing to the block schedule, beginning with "The Origin of the AB Block Schedule at Shadle Park High School, followed by "The implementation of the AB Block Schedule" and "Teacher Training." The second area, "Teachers in the Change Process," presents a variety of teachers' reactions to the change process, along with a section dealing with a "Tragedy for the Staff." The third area is "Relationships between Teachers and Students in the Change Process." The fourth area describes "Teachers' Involvement in Inservice and Training." The fifth area of this chapter, the "Role of Administration in Facilitating This Change," contains the following subheadings: "Collegial Decision-making," "Operational Needs," "Hiring Process," "Teacher Evaluations," and "Collegial Communication."

Initial Stages of Changing to the Block Schedule

Shadle Park High School had been in a scheduling flux since the 1993-94 school year, when the schedule consisted of a traditional six-period day, and when the idea of changing to a block schedule arose for the 1995-96 school year, staff, students, and parents were not in agreement that another change of schedule was in the best interest of the school.

Origin of the AB Block Schedule for Shadle Park High School

According to Amy, an administrator who had been a teacher in this school prior to becoming an administrator, four years ago, several teachers attended a conference in [Metropolis] that included presentations on block scheduling. "Two teachers attended a session on the AB block schedule, and a few others and I went to the four-period day block schedule session. Following the sessions, we discussed the good points and drawbacks of the schedules. During our discussion, a teacher from another school joined us and pointed out the positive experiences her school had with the form of the AB block schedule. That started us thinking in the block schedule direction."

The following year, counselors from Shadle Park High School visited other schools, searching specifically for programs dealing with at-risk grade nine students. Among the topics they targeted were programs to help at-risk students, homeroom programs, school-to-work programs, and advisory programs. According to Amy (one of the two administrators interviewed for this study), "When the counselors came back, they were very excited about the schedules in three of the four schools they had visited. These three schools had gone to various forms of block schedules." The counselors shared their excitement with other teachers and indicated that the larger blocks of time helped solve some of the issues the counselors wanted to resolve related to at-risk students. By creating a schedule with fewer classes and longer time periods each day, the counselors felt students would be under less stress than having six or seven classes to deal with on a daily basis. Counselors also noted that the teachers would meet with fewer students daily and would have more quality time with their students.

According to Amy, a combination of the counselors' visitations and the teachers attending the conference in Metropolis prompted the principal at that time to set up a committee to review scheduling options. One member of this committee recalled: "We seemed to spin our wheels in our lack of focus. A few committee members wanted to look at one schedule model; others wanted to examine only a different, specific block schedule. Other members did not want a block schedule of any kind. When we talked to the staff about block scheduling, we put out too much information, which seemed to confuse and frustrate them. We had talked about going to a block schedule the next school year, but when we presented it to the site council, several people, including teachers, students, and parents, voiced concerns against implementing a block schedule at that time."

Mark, a member of the original committee researching block scheduling, stated, "The principal tried to push the block schedule, then backed off and let the teachers do their research, giving his support for whatever the teachers came up with." Mark indicated that administrative support without demands for a specific plan directed by the principal gave the committee decision-making power that lifted their attitudes about finding a schedule that would work for all teachers. Having a multitude of options, however, contributed to confusion about which schedule to choose."

According to Mark, "The people on the committee were not able to direct their energy toward a plan on which they could agree. As a result, they could not present a plan to the site council that was concise or clearly in the best interest of students." Among those present at the site council meeting were several students who would be seniors the following year. These students pointed out that if the schedule changed again, it would be the third time in their high school years that they would have to adjust to a different schedule. The future seniors present did not want to adjust again. One administrator described the attitude among members of the site council and among those attending the meeting as "negative" toward the change to a block schedule. Members of the scheduling committee decided, according to a committee member, "to back off and look at it for another year."

Amy stated, "We really needed to back off because, if we pushed it and it was turned down, it could be abandoned permanently." The scheduling committee decided to continue studying the issue for another year and focus on the AB block schedule. By directing their attention to one form of schedule, they could be more specific in sharing information with others and more focused on the end result they hoped to achieve. A committee member pointed out that the newly targeted direction of the committee caused the following result: Some members of the committee quit when the AB block schedule became the focus of the majority of the group. As a committee, the group wanted to seek funding for this type of scheduling only, and a few members were opposed to either the AB block or any block schedule. I think they felt alienated from the group, so they just quit. We had to have a focus, so the majority of us went for it, and the membership of the committee changed.

The scheduling committee sought funding from a State Learning Improvement Grant, which Shadle Park High School received from the state. Using this funding to pay for travel and substitute teachers, groups of teachers visited schools with block schedules in place to learn to function in this type of schedule. John, the other administrator, interviewed for this study, remarked that if the teachers could see how the block schedule worked and talk with other teachers about it, these teachers would come back and share their experiences with other teachers. According to this administrator: "There were about 10 or 15 members of the scheduling committee convinced that the AB block schedule was the one we needed to adopt. We hoped that sending 30 teachers to witness this schedule in process at other schools would convince most of them that it would work. Being able to talk with other teachers in their individual departments would help them see how they could apply it themselves. These teachers would return to our school and disseminate the answers to other teachers' questions".

John explained that teachers from schools using the AB block schedule were brought to meet with teachers in their specific departments at Shadle Park High School. Visiting teachers shared how the AB block schedule worked for them in their subject area. In small group settings, a few math teachers, for example, could talk with one math teacher who had experience in the block schedule, and they could discuss the positive and negative aspects of teaching in the block. One committee member stated, "That's [visitations] what won over the vast majority of people to really give the AB block a try."

According to John, after the year of visitations and study of the AB block schedule, the scheduling committee was ready to present their recommendation to the full teaching staff for a decision to put it in place for the 1996-97 school year. The final schedule selected was a modified AB block format. Four days per week would have three 100-minute classes alternating every other day, and one day each week, all six classes would meet for 50-minute classes. This decision was not reached without turmoil.

According to Amy, "By introducing several types of schedules for the vote, those doing the introduction knew the obvious result would be that no one schedule would get enough votes to be selected. A petition which is provided in our charter overruled the initial vote because people said it wasn't fair. It was decided that we would take the top three vote-getters, and we would have a preliminary vote, then a final vote. Then it worked out. People were accusing each other of trying to undermine the governance process. It was very, very uncomfortable."

Although Amy pointed out that getting the final decision was not easy and caused an uncomfortable atmosphere, she also indicated, "Once we decided to do it, people were nice to each other again. It was really energizing to go through that crisis and then come out of it—like a family that had been through the trenches and fought—and then, all of a sudden, happy again.

Implementation of the AB Block Schedule

Once the teaching staff, with the endorsement of the site council, had voted to adopt the block schedule, the process of setting up the roster of classes, registering students, organizing the time frame, and preparing to operate the school for the next year became the focus of concern. Counselors and administrators worked on the master schedule and registering students. The different time frames caused some replanning of assemblies, lunch schedules, school-to-work transition programs, and special needs programs. Once the schedule was put into place, unforeseen problems arose that had to be addressed during the school year.

John, an administrator, stated, "Having pep-cons [pep assemblies] on Fridays was common in the seven-period schedule. In the block schedule, following that format would reduce Wednesday-Friday class time more than Tuesday-Thursday class time. We simply alternated the assemblies equitably. We just hadn't thought about it in advance."

As time conflicts arose, the teachers and administrators worked to minimize the effects on student learning time.

Shadle Park High School is part of the Spokane School District, and with the adoption of the block schedule, the district also had to make accommodations for the many meetings that conflicted with the schedule. According to both administrators, curriculum meetings could take teachers from the same learning-teaching block every two weeks or each month without adversely affecting the student learning time. Administration meetings were altered district-wide to provide the Shadle Park High School administrators the time they needed in their building for administration meetings, departmental meetings, and other activities that depended on the consistency of the block schedule. John commented, "The district was not aware of the potential effect on the overall district, but as the individual building needs arose, the district worked with the building requirements and made adjustments. The district administration was cooperative and supportive of our program.

Teacher Training

The teachers had the opportunity to train for 100-minute class periods by participating in departmental training sessions during the summer. Each department helped organize their own training, and all teachers accepted responsibility for attending, learning, and preparing to augment new techniques in their classrooms. One teacher, Corina, attended the training and planned the first full quarter of lessons during the summer because of her fear of failure.

Corina stated, "During the summer, I attended training sessions, yet the fear kept growing that I would simply not be able to do this. I was considering transferring to another school, even though I wanted to remain here—my own alma mater. The summer training introduced me to project ideas and active group ideas, and some of them seemed possible. I planned the first quarter's lessons. I timed each lesson to the minute. I knew what I was going to do, but I was fearful."

Lois, another teacher, stated, "I was part of a team of teachers who met six times during the summer. We bought timers and planned lessons together to the minute for the entire period of each day."

Many teachers took advantage of the summer training to work with colleagues and on their own to prepare for the block time frame. Some teachers openly shared that they were worried, others admitted to apprehension, and still, others were excited that this type of scheduling had finally arrived. Tim, a teacher with over ten years of experience, shared, "Everything I have learned about teaching in my subject area for the last ten years fits the block schedule, and I am glad it is finally here."

Training was an ongoing process at Shadle Park High School, and consideration of the 100-minute periods had an impact on what administrators and teachers selected for staff development opportunities. John stated, "In the past, we would look for topics of interest to the staff. We still look for timely and interesting, appropriate topics, but we now want trainers who can show us how to adapt and apply topics of interest in our schedule."

One training session for the math department was not a positive experience for the trainer, according to Amy, "The math department, at one point, was very much opposed to the block schedule, and when a woman came in to talk to the group of math teachers, the teachers tended to argue with her about the block scheduling path rather than listen to her presentation. Apparently, she was not that great of a speaker. The lady left in tears, and it was a very bad, bad situation."

Getting quality trainers and training is not easy, as Amy explained. Investigating how trainers have done with other groups, seeking out quality programs, and getting teachers to help select the training programs they think will help them are all suggestions Amy offered to assist in preventing unproductive situations.

Amy had been a teacher during the planning and training sessions prior to her becoming an administrator and prior to the school moving to the block schedule. She had been trained along with the English teachers. She stated, "I had gone through all of the training, and I personally felt really prepared. I knew that as an English department, we had done lots of planning and had an expert help us reach our confidence level. When I became an administrator, I realized that not all departments had experienced as effective training as we had received. When I started visiting teachers' classrooms, my perception of them before the change was that they had been good teachers, but now they were having problems. I asked them, "Didn't you learn about energizers?" No, they had not. They were not trained well enough to deal with the time adjustments either. Even though people were really trying, they were flat-out scared."

Amy became an administrator in the first year of the block schedule, and she did not teach in this schedule. She recalled teachers coming to her the first few days of school expressing both their terror and their excitement about the new schedule. Amy described the schedule's first September as a honeymoon period.

Amy noted, "Teachers said things like, 'Oh, we love it!' and 'Oh, it's so much better!' but by the end of September, all of their lesson plans that they had put together during the summer had run out. Really, this literally happened. I am not exaggerating. They had planned all the way through the month of September, thinking, I've got to get September planned because I'll be too busy. Well, then, all of a sudden, September ended, and we had another month of—several months of planning to go. They were really starting to take a dive."

Teachers began to grasp the change that they were facing once they were into it and experiencing it. According to both John and Amy, the teachers at their different levels of preparation began to experience high levels of stress as the school year moved into October.

In recalling my experience at Kettle Falls High School, I believe I was fortunate not having the level of conflict in putting together a scheduling committee as Shadle Park High School experienced. Perhaps the smaller school size contributed to the ease of getting a committee together. Our method of selection did not allow for volunteers, and that may have facilitated the process.

whwhwhwhwhwhwhwhwhwhwhwhwhwhwhwhwhwhwhwhwhwhwhwhwhwhwh

What Happened?

Coach Carter

Coach Carter, a film starring Samuel Jackson and directed by Thomas Carter, is an absolute "must-see" for anyone considering or participating in a transition to a block schedule–or any major change in education.

Background: Coach Carter, the newly hired coach and former student of this high school, had an amazing background in professional coaching, and as a "corrective action," he was assigned to coach at his own former high school. He came in with a passion, a plan, and his own bulldozer attitude to inflict his plan on everyone in the school. Basketball team students were his first targets, parents next, then administration and teaching staff. When the film ends, it is clear that Coach Carter really had his students' well-being and success as his priority, and so much of what he wanted to do was amazing.

What happened? Coach Carter, in carrying out his plans, did not bring anyone up to speed to work with him prior to setting his plans in place. His actions placed demands on students, their parents, teachers, and the community. His demands did not consider the whole organization and how his plan could fit into the overall operation of the school. As a result, everyone (according to Carter) needed to follow Carter's plan, and he expected the administrators and the school board to back all of his ideas and actions—AND Coach Carter was not diplomatic about it. Of course, this makes for an excellent plot for a film—based on a true situation—and an exciting film.

What could have happened? Coach Carter could have met with administrators prior to his enforcing his plans to make sure they were on board with his program. This would give them opportunities to discuss, suggest, and learn about it prior to the organic material hitting the ventilating device. He could have met with parents and given a complete explanation of how his practices work, what his expectations were of students and parents, and how they could support his students/their children in this amazing team transition from failure to exceptional. He could have met with teachers before the season started to explain his views on the importance of academic success in playing basketball and what he expected the teachers to do about it—what their time commitment would be, and how he expected them to communicate with him. He did not do that. Many participants felt blind-sided, disrespected, and angry.

What did happen? The expression "All hell broke loose" fits well. Change is hard, especially for the people who feel forced to make the changes. Forced or unwelcome change, regardless of the good it can do if it actually takes place, can tear an organization apart. I strongly urge readers and anyone who is planning on making changes that require action and acceptance from others to ***watch this film first***. If you are already in the middle of a change process, you will enjoy it even more. Coach Carter is an amazing man, and his idealistic devotion to getting his team members to become successful on the court and in life was admirable. His approach to making others change, however, without their prior input or permission, had its consequences. Change is tough enough when a person agrees to it, but when blind-sided, it can be painful. I believe Coach Carter could have executed his plans respectfully. So can we.

whwhwhwhwhwhwhwhwhwhwhwhwhwhwhwhwhwhwhwhwhwhwhwhwh

Teachers in the Change Process

Teachers who dialogued about their professional adjustments and changes in moving to the block schedule included their emotional responses in an integral way. Lois, a teacher, explained her professional insecurity, "I felt awkward instead of in charge and confident as I had always felt before, and I did not like feeling that way. I talked with others with similar feelings. It was as though I were a new teacher again, and I was uncomfortable. Being forced to change meant growth for me." Lois had been a teacher for 20 years. She admitted to being challenged more than she expected, and it was both uncomfortable and awkward.

Harrison prided himself on being an excellent, animated lecturer who kept students on task easily in the 50-minute period. He explained, "I was animated, used demonstrations, humor, and I held students' attention because I knew the material well, and it was easy for me to present to students. Now I have many more papers to grade. Group work seems ineffective with the typical arrangement of a bright student, a slow student, and a couple of average students. Bright ones care, slow ones are unproductive—some do nothing and don't care to try. If I could have my wish, I would have 28 students on the ninth grade level all by myself. It would be better if students have fewer teachers and really get to know their teachers. They [students] just don't know how to relate to people."

Jerry had previous experience with the block schedule prior to coming to Shadle Park High School. Jerry explained, "I was used to classes lasting two hours each, so this schedule was not difficult for me to adjust to. It forces teachers to be more prepared for lessons, planning all parts of the time frame." Planning has been a topic for all of the teachers with whom I dialogued. Whether planning lesson plans had become easier or more difficult to develop, teachers interviewed agreed that it is definitely different and requires both professional and personal adjustments with the movement to the block schedule.

Roger experienced a personal and professional loss with the change. He stated, "Large music programs are not workable in block schedules. Music has been shown through the test of time to need practice every day. When I asked a coach if every other day was enough for football or basketball practice, the coach's answer was laughter. Meeting daily builds skills. It is professionally frustrating. I stay because I feel I will do the least amount of damage. I'm the logical one to make it work. I went from being one of the top teachers in the area to being a troublemaker because I opposed the switch. I was excluded last year from any decision-making. Administrators and boards need to do their homework and learn to recognize the uniqueness of the arts and music. Music is made the center of the curriculum where it is scheduled successfully."

Roger shared that he did not embrace the schedule at the time of adoption, nor does he support it in its second year. In discussing the role of music in scheduling, he preferred the seven-period day because the students met and practiced music daily. Daily practice, according to this music teacher, is essential for success in music.

Keith was supportive and adjusted easily in the area of special needs: "Our curriculum is really functional, so we have to be very flexible, to begin with. Our focus is directed toward the transition to life and after high school for our uniquely challenged, mildly retarded young adults." Keith was particularly pleased to see the teaching staff embrace the block schedule. He stated, "It's been really amazing to me. I never thought I would see the positive approach and that people really seemed to buy into it. It did create more of a challenge for people who have had more of a traditional classroom setting because they had to rethink their approach to things. I think sometimes we need some change anyway. We seem to get into ruts, and it helped to shape people up a little bit and to take a different look at things."

The teachers in this study experienced a variety of professional and personal responses to the change, as their comments have indicated. Corina expressed a contrast in a professional and personal response to the change that was vivid. Corina explained, "Before the first day, I had trouble sleeping, and when school actually started, my trauma worsened. The thought of what I would do with these students for 100 minutes was frightening. I was adamantly opposed to the change, vocal to anyone who would listen, and ready to change my life—even give up teaching—out of fear of failure. The pain I experienced was deep, long-lasting, and real. Knowing that, I must say that I would not want to return to the traditional schedule. The loudest dissenter would not want to return to what I tried to preserve so strongly. This is my 24th year of teaching. I have proven that I can grow, change, and make my classes better through varied teaching techniques. I am a better teacher and a stronger person for what I have experienced."

The teachers shared a common description of their first year's experience with the block schedule: they felt like they were starting over. For some of them, feeling like a beginner again after many years of experience was uncomfortable, frightening, and even painful. The adjustment for some teachers was minor; for others, dramatic. Ann, who had served on the scheduling committee and who had supported the block schedule change throughout the process, responded, "When the results of the vote from the staff were posted to move to this schedule, I was having a few tears and second, or reflective, thoughts. The principal asked me why. I began to realize that I was going to have to change, and I was unsure of how successful I would be in making that change. The emotion of realizing that it was truly happening—and happening to me—was intense."

In discussing how this would affect Ann's teaching, she said that she felt that she could be great in a block schedule. Ann said, "I was an excellent teacher. I felt that I could be great in the block schedule. I am good now and growing better with practice. I have discovered that I am reaffirmed as a professional educator. After 25 years of teaching a certain way, I learned that I can change and grow. I am proud of my ability to meet this challenge—and it was a challenge—and it continues to be a challenge every day."

Ann explained that she worked throughout the summer prior to the change, preparing herself to meet the challenges of the block schedule. She and other teachers have agreed that it takes actually being in the schedule itself on a daily basis to really grasp the impact of the change on a person's teaching style.

As September turned into October and some teachers had run out of the lesson plans they had prepared during the summer, Amy noticed that she had teachers coming to her complaining about a variety of issues. Amy stated, "Some teachers complained that they were stressed by the change required of them in block scheduling and not having time to plan. Teachers who had never complained in the past would be in my office complaining about something an administrator did, or their department head had done. Colleagues would get into fights with one another to the point where one of them would be in tears. We are just not that type of staff. I think we are a very cohesive staff."

Amy shared an experience with one teacher who had been one of her good friends on staff. "I had a department head come to my office who is one of my good friends, and still is, and just rant and rave about several things. I literally took a list. "Number 1, okay," and I repeated it back to her. "You're upset about this. Okay. There were ten things that this department head was upset about, and I just took it all down and I said, 'I'll try to work on it.' Afterward, I thought, this is the oddest conversation I have ever had with her. I found myself getting very upset. I was afraid the staff was honestly going to blow up at each other or at us."

Amy shared her concerns with John about the teachers' tension, complaints, and anger. As a result of Amy's concerns, a consultant who specialized in organizational change and its effects came to Shadle Park High School to help find solutions and a return to the previous cohesion the staff had prior to the schedule change. The consultant, according to Amy, indicated that the honeymoon period was over and that the staff was now in crisis. In order to work with the teachers, the consultant agreed to come to a teachers' meeting in early November.

Tragedy for the Staff

Amy set up the teachers' meeting, but the format of the meeting did not occur as planned due to a tragic incident. Amy explained, "On Halloween, our senior class president committed suicide, and that put the school into another crisis mode. Talking about organizational change four days later was not going to cut it." The meeting still took place, and the consultant directed a discussion about suicide and the impact it had on both students and staff. John and Amy concurred that an incident such as this has a strong effect on both students and teachers. As a result, the focus of confusion, anger, and frustration that had been directed toward the schedule, according to both John and Amy, seemed to become insignificant compared to their feelings about the student's unexpected death.

Amy stated, "All of a sudden, I think people really came together as a staff because of the suicide. I think people started to realize that what we had been going through was nothing compared to this. People started loosening up a little. When in December I brought the consultant back, it really fell flat because we were through that and ready to move on.

Both Amy and John indicated that the whole focus on the block schedule changed after the suicide. By winter break, the teachers with whom I dialogued generally agreed that the teachers were exhausted. One person stated, "People weren't mean to each other anymore, and just about everyone admitted to being tired." Following the winter break, the attitude was positive, the tension of the previous months seemed gone, and teachers were directing their energy toward teaching, according to several of the teachers with whom I dialogued.

Another tragedy came to Shadle Park High school with the death of a counselor who had served the district for many years. Amy noted, "There were so few things that worked well last year because of the suicide, and then the counselor dying. It was just such a weird year anyway. It was a learning year, a grieving year, and few things worked well."

My experience in Kettle Falls did not include the tragedies of losing a high-profile student and the death of a long-serving counselor. Individual problems arose, including a teacher discovering breast cancer who faced year-long treatment, another teacher experiencing ill health, which led to serious heart problems and eventual surgery, and the accidental death of a student in a car accident. Though tragic, none of these incidents had a deep impact on all staff members at once. Two health issues, however, deeply impacted the two teachers, their families, and their close friends on an ongoing basis, so the impact on some people was deeply felt, and others may have experienced a minor impact. Of course, when a student passes at so young an age, the entire staff and I grieved for this loss privately and daily.

At Kettle Falls, I experienced a strong connection with the two medically challenged teachers as I worked with them in their classes and as they implemented a variety of teaching techniques. They both enriched the staff as we learned to assist more kindly through their tears, their physical pain, and their emotional bouts with illness and change as success, or lack of it, touched them in our work together. No day went by without my feeling for them.

Relationships between Teachers and Students in the Change Process

A block schedule impacts teachers in their planning and delivery of lessons, as the previous information relates. Teachers experienced some specific changes, and students participated in these changes as well. Lois related her feelings about her students and the various reactions to her math classes: "Having to adapt to a new time frame allowed more time for activities. I had wanted to do a quilt activity for five years, but I was never able to get it into the plan." Lois had a quilt attached to the wall in her room. For her students, this project included designing through geometry assignments, and then students carried out the design by constructing a quilt. Teams of students worked on the many phases of the project. Lois explained, "The class was involved in designing with a geometric stipulation, and there was a cutting team and a sewing team. The students chose the design from several designs other students had created. Having more flexibility with time was helpful to Lois, yet the change was not easy for her:

According to Lois, "It had been a major difficult change, but I would not want to teach in the old schedule again. I have always been positive in relating to a student. That is easier now. I used to think—did I touch base with that student? I am more relaxed now because I make contact with every student easily in the longer block."

Lois explained that her calculus students seemed able to stay on task for the entire period and wondered where the time went. Geometry students required her to make more effort to get students motivated and to stay on task.

Tim, a teacher who had also been involved in coaching, stated, "Students are different from what they were even five years ago. Some stare listlessly or tune out, regardless of the effort a teacher puts into planning and delivery." In comparing teaching to coaching, Tim explained, "I have definite expectations of football team members. We drill until they get it. This is lacking today. Teachers don't follow through with accountability. Some teachers don't know what they want." For Tim, an important factor in his acceptance of the block schedule had to do with relationship building. Tim stated, "I believe there are three things a teacher must do: know the student's name, know the student, and hold the student accountable for learning—make sure the student learns. It is better that students have fewer teachers and really get to know the teachers. Students just don't know how to relate to people."

Mark, a teacher in the vocational area, expressed his appreciation for the longer time period the block schedule provided. "Today I'm taking my class to work on the Habitat for Humanities project during the next block. They stay through lunch, and the students who have early work release classes stay until 2:00 p.m. Students gain a positive experience due to a long enough period of time. It isn't realistic to work on a house in a 50-minute period. Getting there and doing anything just isn't realistic."

In regard to planning, Mark also stated, "It forces teachers to be more prepared for lessons, planning all parts of the time frame. I thought it would work well and meet students' needs for a variety of classes. It didn't work for some—too rushed or too much non-directed time—some students didn't respond to some classes and did nothing, and some teachers didn't plan effectively."

Amy, in relating her experience with teachers and lesson planning, explained, "Some teachers who thought they would not need to change their lesson planning did have to change, and others who were sure they would have to change, didn't." Amy explained, "One teacher, in particular, was just a great dynamic teacher, really fabulous in the classroom, and his students really got involved in the 50-minute period. His kids were complaining about him because he was using the lecture strategy for 100 minutes. The kids were dying in a longer time frame."

As an administrator observing many teachers, Amy noted that more teachers were bringing hands-on things, such as markers, pens, and poster activities, and trying to do more energizers or activities that get students out of their seats or at least more actively involved in their learning. Amy's perception was that in classes where teachers involved students actively in learning activities, students liked the block schedule. In classes where they were passive learners, they did not indicate liking the schedule. Amy stated, "This year I have a bigger distinction in my mind between block schedule issues and teaching issues. Last year I could observe a lesson and say—something's off here. Kids started talking at the end of the lesson and so it was more vague. I didn't necessarily put a name on it. For example, one teacher from a different district, new to our school last year, had good ideas, lots of lessons, but her transitions were rough. She tried five transitions, and she didn't have to do that in a 50-minute period. That is a block schedule issue."

When teachers have problems moving from one activity to another, students lose their continuity as well, according to Jane, a teacher who had lectured in the 50-minute period. Jane remarked, "It took a while for me to get the hang of it, and students helped me make the adjustment. I quit focusing on myself, and I began focusing on them and their need for continuity. In other words, I quit thinking, 'What am I going to do next that is organized for me?' I would think, 'How will the students move from one point to another in a way that makes sense to them?' The focus on students is really the key that makes the block schedule work."

John, as an administrator, noted that elementary teachers could be of help to some teachers in learning how to transition well. He pointed out that elementary teachers use transitions throughout each day with the same groups of students. John stated, "A good elementary teacher could model as many as 20 or more transitions in one day. Seeing that would help secondary teachers get the hang of shifting from one point to another in their lessons."

Looking for the organization of the school from the student's standpoint was important to John. "Think about what a student has to do in seven periods—meet seven teachers' requirements, assignments, and class rules. At least four days a week with the block schedule, the student has three teachers to deal with. And then, of course, teachers focus on two or three classes of students. It has to be less stressful and less complicated just by limiting the number of people and sets of directions each side [students and teachers] has to deal with."

Students and teachers have a better chance of positive rapport with the block schedule, according to Lois, but she pointed out that it can also work the other way. "If things aren't clicking in a good way between a student and a teacher, a 100-minute period can get pretty long for both of them. It forces us to work harder on relationship building, but we are not always successful."

Other teachers agreed that a student might be overlooked in a 50-minute period, but not so in a 100-minute period. Teachers seem to have time to make contact with each student in some way. Ann also indicated, "The focus for high school teachers here is now moving toward students as their first responsibility, and the subject or material as the second. We're really here for students, so it's a great thing."

Time became vital in preparing and delivering lessons, according to Jerry. He explained, "I used to just talk until the bell rang, and I didn't think much about the kids. Now I plan two-to-four different sections with activities I think will keep the kids on task. I watch to see if the time frame is working, and I adjust if the kids aren't responding. The old way was easier for all of us—teachers and kids, but the longer period is more challenging for all of us—harder but better. Nobody gets to drift along if they're doing this thing right."

Both teachers and administrators acknowledged that the students were not actively involved in the planning or development of the block schedule at Shadle Park High School. According to Ann, the teachers were the ones who had to make it work, and they had to be the ones who planned it. Amy indicated, "I think it's a more humane schedule, and if it's more humane for the adults, then they're going to treat the kids better. I think the kids do equally well, if not better, in the block schedule. It allows them to think more deeply in areas like English and social studies. Students flat out do better. In some subjects, I'm not sure if they do better with the every-other-day schedule. Some teachers have said freshmen and sophomores in pre-algebra, for example, can't seem to stay focused or remember their assignments with the every-other-day plan—they don't accept accountability or responsibility well."

The teachers at Kettle Falls High School experienced many of the emotional reactions and preparation problems that Shadle Park High School teachers experienced. I knew the teachers were having problems, and I discussed their problems with them at length. But not until I listened intently to the Shadle Park High School teachers did I begin to fully grasp the Kettle Falls teachers' frustration and pain. I wish I could go back in time and listen more empathetically to my colleagues, assure them that they were professionally on track, and give them personal support and professional help to a greater degree than I did.

I also shared many hours discussing with students their concerns about boring, long-winded, lecturing teachers whom they endured just fine with a shorter time frame. Long periods seemed hard on both lecturing teachers and listening—or trying to listen—students. Enlightening the teachers who were the topics of these discussions was not an easy task, but nonetheless, an essential task for their growth and for students' sake. I could see the change was very difficult for some teachers and not as hard for others.

The administrative role in the process does not seem to provide the same daily challenge every class period as does the teacher role. I believe I was caring and supportive, yet I now believe that until I serve as the teacher in the classroom, I will not fully appreciate their sacrifice, their pain, and grief, or their confusion and, in some cases, their loss of self-esteem.

whwhwhwhwhwhwhwhwhwhwhwhwhwhwhwhwhwhwhwhwhwhwhwhwhwhwhwh

What Happened?

Boy Code

As educators, we must find the time to learn about our students, understand them, and protect them. When our high school classes are too large, our total student load is 170 - 190 students per day, that necessity becomes impossible—

but we must do it. I hesitate to know what could have been the outcome for Rick if his teacher had not helped him.

Background of Boy Code: Freshman English in this small high school brought together fourteen boys and fifteen girls who were new to high school, apprehensive about their new status, and worried about fitting in, managing the workload, and finding their way through the halls with bigger students surrounding them. In addition to the rest of the student body, they had each other to continue through school, and their middle school experiences held some basic rules among themselves. Perhaps one of the strongest ones affecting them was the Boy Code.

On the first day of class, Mrs. Thomas introduced herself, the new teacher in school.

She told them five things about herself, and then she asked them to write a paragraph using five sentences that told her about them as students here in school. To begin their writing, she asked them to think about what questions they might ask someone whom they had just met. She gave them some examples: "What name do you like to be called?" "What do you like best about school?" "What causes you to worry about school?" "Do you participate in an after-school activity?" (and their own preferred topics). She told them that she might share these with their parents and the class (to ensure appropriate questions and answers). After class, Rick asked her a question after all of the other students had left the room.

"What if I don't like school?" His voice was soft, and clear, and he looked at the floor as he waited for an answer.

"Don't you like anything about school?" Mrs. Thomas asked.

"No. and if I write that, and you read it out loud, it won't go good for me." He looked into my eyes. Then he again stared at the floor.

"Why don't you write the things about your life that you feel safe telling anyone? You can describe where you live, your favorite relative or friend, any hobbies you have, or a pet you have now or used to have. You can tell something that you have imagined."

Rick looked relieved. "You won't read my paper out loud in class?"

"Not unless you want me to," she smiled. "What's your name?"

"Rick. I'm Richard, but I go by Rick." He stood uncomfortably by her desk, waiting for —what? She waited, too. Maybe he needed some time to form a sentence—time to think.

"Do you like to write, Rick?"

"Sometimes. I don't like others to read it, especially other kids."

"Why?"

"You'll figure it out when you're here awhile. I gotta go." He left the room.

She heard scuffling noises in the hall, and when she stepped out to investigate, she saw two boys roughly holding onto Rick's arms, pushing him up against the wall. When they saw Mrs. Thomas, they let go of Rick and took off.

"Rick, did they hurt you?" She was very concerned.

"Not this time. You opened the door." He was trying to hold back tears that refused to be held. "Sorry. Boys don't cry, right?" He cried. "I hate it here." She brought him back into her classroom so he could cry without others seeing him. He sat at an empty desk, put his head down, and tried to stop crying. She went to her desk and gave him time to settle down. After a few moments, he said a soft goodbye and moved slowly toward the door.

Then What Happened? "You are welcome here anytime, Rick, even if I'm not in my room. Just come in." Mrs. Thomas said to him in a gentle manner.

"Really?" He paused briefly. "Like, during lunch? After school?"

"Yes—anytime you need to. Even if I'm having class, just take a seat in the back like you belong there. Read a book, do some homework—whatever seems right." Rick was silent, looking hard into my eyes, like he was waiting for something, but she didn't know what.

"Okay. Thank you." He left my room, watching her as he eased out the door.

Days and weeks went by with Rick stopping in at lunchtime, before and after school, quietly sitting at a back-row desk doing homework. Two or three times a week, he calmly entered her classroom and moved to the back of the room, sitting near the large bookshelves with a book of his own, or he would read one from the shelf. He would leave quietly when he chose with an 'anytime' pass she had given him so he could get into his next class late. They didn't talk often or have open conversations about his life, but she noticed that he smiled much more as time went on.

Rick's composition work in Freshman English had gradually become more creative. His characters often resembled other students, and their actions resembled the actual situations that had occurred in school or in the community. After a theft had occurred, Rick wrote an extra-credit short story about two boys who had robbed the local drug store. He included details about what was taken, including the names of specific drugs, tools, and snacks that Mrs. Thomas later learned were actually part of the robbery.

Several of Rick's earlier essays and stories had included paragraphs that described bullying incidents in school, naming specific students (including his own name). Mrs. Thomas clearly understood why Rick did not want her to read his assignments in class. She had told the principal what a student had told her in confidence, and he found the information credible, leading to disciplinary action for a few of the students.

Rick was using Mrs. Thomas to fight his bully battles. Why else would he tell her and even remind her not to read his papers in class? The robbery was just too big an event in a small town for Mrs. Thomas not to share Rick's information with the local sheriff. She wrote some notes based on Rick's robbery details so she wouldn't have to expose him as the one who gave her this information, and she shared it with the sheriff. The details Rick had given her and that she shared with the sheriff brought about the search of both boys' homes, their arrest, and their conviction. The boys were sent to a detention facility far from home.

Rick's visits to her classroom gradually decreased. He stopped in after school one day. "Do you have a few minutes to talk?" He had a smile and a twinkle in his eyes.

"Yes, I have time," she said. "I've been hoping you would want to visit a bit. Your creative writing has been interesting, to say the least. Do you have any thoughts on how you came up with some of your ideas?" She had to ask him.

"Thank you for giving me a safe place to be in school. When school started, I was sure I wouldn't make it through the year with all the bullying I was dealing with. The boys that did the robbery? Well, they beat me up every chance they got."

"Why didn't you tell the principal—or someone—me? Your parents?" she asked.

"These guys would just get detention or something if anyone would believe me, and then they'd get me big time for telling on them. They called me 'gay,' and "faggot" and all sorts of names like that. When I found out they robbed the store, it was the right time to get them out of town for a long time. Did you take my paper to the sheriff?"

"No. I took your information to the sheriff. I didn't say who had given it to me. The sheriff searched the boys' homes and found the drugs and other things," she told him. How did you find out that they robbed the store?"

"The last time they beat me up, they thought they had knocked me out. They thought it was funny, but they didn't know that I could hear every word they said. I just laid there and listened. They took some of the pills they stole, talked about the names of the pills, which ones worked best, and went on and on about what they stole, getting high and acting weird. I just stayed still, listened, and memorized the names of the drugs by saying them over and over in my head. They left me there and went away laughing."

"Where were you?"

"In the alley behind the gym." We were both quiet for a bit. "I am gay."

"How do you know that?" she asked him.

"I've known for a long time. I tried not to be, but I am. That's why I get beat up. It's like 'boy code'—boys beat up boys who are gay—and that's okay."

"Has anyone ever told you that it's okay to be gay?" she asked. He looked at her with wide, questioning eyes. "It is okay to be gay—and not get beat up."

"Nobody ever said that to me. My dad hates me for not going out for basketball. I don't measure up, he says. I'm weak. I'm an embarrassment to him."

Rick broke down crying. "A few times, Dad yelled at me, 'Don't act like a fag!'"

After a few moments, she said, "Listen to me. You have a right to be gay. You have a right to be safe in school and everywhere else. You have a right not to be beaten by anyone. You have a right to take charge of your life and never allow anyone to ever beat you or mistreat you again." Mrs. Thomas sat near him and held his hand as tears fell softly.

"Those boys are out of here for a while, but there are others like them just as mean and unfair as they are. I will help you all I can, but you need to help yourself—and others. You can help other people that are mistreated. Be with people you can trust."

Update on Rick: Rick graduated from high school and college, and became a teacher of religious faith. As a teenager, he was sexually abused by a religious leader, threatened by that person that Rick would suffer terribly if he told on him—and that no one would believe him anyway. Years later, that abuser was convicted of many counts of sexual abuse. Rick suffered at the evil hands of others. He is now openly gay and an advocate for others who face the same discrimination and violence that he faced. The "Boy Code" could have killed him as a freshman in high school. Now he saves other boys from this unfair, widespread 'code' that means, 'If you are gay, you get tortured.'

How does this relate to this book: When teachers get to know students, they can protect them, find ways to keep them safe in school, and help them develop courage, feel safe, and be successful students. These students with personal issues need connections with adults who will help them be confident students—and become confident adults.

whwhwhwhwhwhwhwhwhwhwhwhwhwhwhwhwhwhwhwhwhwhwhwhwhwh

Teachers' Involvement in Inservice and Training

Training was an essential factor for teachers to implement the block schedule, according to John, "We had a lot of training the year before the block schedule would go into place. Each department wrote its own proposal as to how they were going to train to prepare to teach in the 100-minute periods. They could identify individuals who would come in and give them ideas, talk about their own experiences, and help the departments process that information. This gave the staff the ability to design and take ownership of the training, and they could make it specifically meet their needs as they saw it."

John explained that the staff designed their own staff development, and the district provided funding through both district funds and grant funds to pay for training. John described the teachers' focus, "It wasn't that they didn't know the content. They wanted to have the assurance that they knew activities and strategies based on content that would give students that deeper level of learning because our Student Learning Improvement Plan focused on extending and applying critical thinking skills."

John explained that Shadle Park High School had eight half-days for professional planning: "We devoted seven of those teaching in the block periods. There was some large group work, some focused group work, but it was on a face-to-face thing—a small group focus. They did the processing of what was working and what wasn't working. They discussed what they now wanted to know, and then they went out and found that out through site visitations to other schools or research—whatever means necessary. We also provided mini-workshops among our staff for people who had energizers. Teachers who had strategies were sharing them with their colleagues."

Tim gave his view of the inservice: "Some inservices were a waste of time. Some teachers really needed effective training. When inservice involved having teachers in our subject areas come in from other block schedule systems, it was helpful."

Amy stated, "The block schedule isn't going to do anything to improve student learning by itself. Because of what it forces teachers to do, it improves teaching—and then it causes learning to improve. Teachers have had training, but the self-training they have done for themselves or on their own has been essential. Taking inservice ideas, applying them, discussing them with colleagues, and trying again in different ways make the difference for teachers. The application and reapplication of training make it work. The change to the block has forced teachers to learn and challenge themselves to be better prepared and more knowledgeable about teaching strategies."

A teacher shared, "This [block schedule] has forced me to be a better teacher than I was before. I have to be better. I have to learn—and train."

A heuristic experience for me involved my participation in training with teachers throughout the year. I appreciate Amy's having participated with the English teachers because I believe she was better prepared to serve teachers and evaluate performance with in-depth training. I learned with the teachers at Kettle Falls, and I shared some learning sessions at Shadle Park High School. I value the training, and I believe I was able to serve Kettle Falls teachers more richly and understand the Shadle Park High School teachers and administrators more thoroughly because of sharing their experiences. I also participated in administrative training during my second year at Kettle Falls, which broadened my knowledge in areas of team development and evaluation. The Educational Service District provided this training for eastern Washington administrators.

Role of Administration in Facilitating This Change

Administrators play an essential role in facilitating change. Administrators may need to provide collegial decision-making opportunities and operational stability, hire effectively, provide positive and risk-free teacher evaluation, and promote collegial communication. Each of these areas may provide insight into the role of administration in restructuring.

Collegial Decision-Making

John, an administrator, discussed the importance of teachers having a decision-making role in the whole process of developing and implementing the schedule change. "The decision to make this change has to be coming from the teachers because they are the ones who actually have to carry it out." John indicated that parents and students would like to have something to say also, but he pointed out that the teachers must have the most important say and that administrators need to make sure that their voices are heard. John stated, "Administrators need to support, encourage, and provide teachers with the time to think through the whole process. Stepping in and taking over just won't work in this kind of change." John pointed out two important areas that administrators can protect to ease the change process for teachers. One area he noted was the protection and provision of teachers with time for collegial sharing, training, and meetings within the school day and with pay when training or important meetings need to occur outside the school day or in the summer.

Operational Needs

Another area involves the operational needs that may challenge or interfere with the operation of the schedule. John explained:

Administrators need to show that the day is not going to be interrupted. The students need to be able to do the same things, and the teachers need to be able to effectively do the same things in terms of offering courses and having the flexibility in the day to mesh with those things outside of school. That means administrators deal with everything from transportation, the master schedule, and all the schedules related to school activities. Other schedules include sports, clubs and activities, band trips, lunchtime, assemblies, and so on.

John was particularly clear on the issue of communication with teachers: "We have to assure the teachers that we are listening to them as we figure out ways acceptable to them that will not be disruptive to classes and their teaching." John explained that in addition to providing order throughout the day, the administration needed to provide a safe environment for change.

A safe environment for teachers, according to John, means a collegial atmosphere where teachers are encouraged to take risks. "We are now more of a learning community where we can all be open to ideas and respectful of each other—really wanting to talk to each other, learn, and share. People have to take a lot of risks. Administrators must provide a safe environment for teachers in order for them to be able to take risks and share their errors as well as their successes. That means the evaluation process cannot be used in such a way that teachers get marked down because they took a chance on a new teaching delivery system or teaching technique.

Hiring Process

Amy indicated that the hiring process requires attention to skills that may not have been as important in the traditional schedule. Amy stated, "Classroom management skills in 50 minutes are different from what they need to be in 100 minutes. We need to bring teachers into our school who can work with other teachers, have the flexibility and the willingness to learn, and who are risk-takers."

In interviewing potential teachers, Amy indicated that the emphasis has changed. "A great teacher in a 50-minute period may not be great in a 100-minute period," Amy stated. She continued, "The block schedule shines a bright spotlight on poor classroom management and poor transitions."

John indicated, "If an applicant does not understand how to transition from one phase of a lesson to another, and many secondary teachers do not, we have to decide if that applicant is open to learning or set in practiced ways." The importance of fitting into the teaching community is essential, according to both John and Amy. Teachers are working hard, both John and Amy have indicated, and other staff members do not have time, nor do they want to deal with non learning, non contributing teachers.

Teacher Evaluation

John and Amy agreed that the evaluation process which administrators use to evaluate teaching performance provides an ongoing opportunity to encourage teachers to develop their teaching skills. According to John:

As administrators, we can take an already stressed teacher who feels like he's drowning in the 100-minute period and demoralize him with criticism of what he is doing wrong. Or we can help him target specific problems and find ways to pull him up to the surface for air. Usually, a teacher in trouble has only one problem— let's say it's not enough variation in activities—or class control (or both). Once we target the problem, we can help the teacher develop techniques and solutions.

Amy noted, "Department meetings regularly also provide collegial support for their members. Administrators need to make the time available for departments to meet. It has to be a meaningful time, and it has to be often."

Collegial Communication

Administrators who have read research on the change process or who have experienced change themselves may be aware that change for teachers is not easy, and in some cases, change can be painful. Corina (the teacher who said that she responded the most of anyone in the emotional sense) stated:

Any school reviewing this type of change will have a teacher like me who refuses to give this a chance. People who have given us workshops and seminars agree that there are always people who fight for change—teachers, parents, administrators, and others.

Although Corina admitted that she was probably the most vocal in trying to defeat the block schedule, she indicated midway through the first year of the new schedule that she would not want to return to the six- or seven-period schedule again. John indicated that his role included keeping dissidents from stopping or blocking the debate on change, as well as keeping those teachers who were adamantly for the change from keeping discussion for everyone open to all views. John stated, "It takes being in tune with teachers and frequent, individual communication so we know where they all are in the thought process."

Amy pointed out that the one thing that worked best was the collaborative period. She stated, "The collaborative period allowed teachers time to work together and administrators time to be out there with teachers as needed." Amy indicated, "I can't say as an administrator I had any great impact on the collaborative time for teachers besides supporting the schedule and supporting the time." When Amy realized the point where teachers were very tired, she stated, "I wish for some of our inservice days we had just said, 'Do what you want because the teachers were so tired. For the most part, they listened politely, but they were exhausted."

Amy, in retrospect, noted, "Schools that make this change should spend the first year taking care of the teachers. I can't stress enough: take care of your staff. Don't plan on any other type of restructuring. Don't start new classes. Just concentrate on the block schedule and devote all of the time you can to giving teachers time to talk to one another about what they are doing. Build in collaborative times because I know that has helped these teachers survive."

Tim indicated that he was concerned about teachers who became frustrated and became ineffective in the classroom. Tim commented, "Some teachers depend on videos too much. They have trouble adjusting to the longer time frame, so they just opt to fill in anything to get through the period. I worry about the total school program and the loss of quality across several areas. The administration needs to take care of this and keep teachers accountable. I use videos myself, but not as a constant crutch or filler—only as pertinent to course work. It would only take a few teachers to damage the quality and reputation of our school.

As Tim has indicated, administrators need to keep in touch with the teachers, and as evaluators of the curriculum and lesson delivery, administrators may need to provide programs of improvement for struggling teachers.

As principal of Kettle Falls High School and as the team leader of a group of teachers in the process of change, I agree with both Amy and John that staff needs time, attention, and a high level of ongoing communication with one another and with administrators. The size of the Kettle Falls staff made frequent communication possible. Our weekly teachers' meetings provided an open forum for expression. Our open forum required an oral commitment from every teacher every week to voice concerns about block scheduling. I believe their frequent sharing kept many small problems from becoming large ones.

Amy and John have a much larger teaching staff to reach, and they take advantage of the other administrators, department chairpersons, and other teacher-leaders to reach a personal level of communication. The success of the block schedule at Kettle Falls rested with the teachers accepting the change, communicating often, and allowing me to lead with their constant guidance.

Summary

Two administrators shared their experiences and their school's process of changing to the block schedule. Ten teachers also gave their personal perspectives of the change process and how they saw their peers' reactions. The early stages of development, planning, and implementation of the block schedule for Shadle Park High School are shared through these twelve people with several levels of involvement in the whole process.

Teachers described their experiences in the change process and noted how the process affected their teaching, their students, their relationships with both colleagues and students, and their impressions of the role administrators need to play in the change process. Administrators explained their perspectives of the teachers in the change process, and they discussed the role administrators may need to fulfill to effectively assist teachers as they move from a traditional teaching model to the unique requirements of the block schedule.

I have shared my personal and professional experiences on topics of committee development, emotional and professional involvement, participation in training, and communication. My involvement with Shadle Park High School teachers and administrators brought me a greater depth of appreciation for teachers involved in the change process during my four-year experience with the Kettle Falls High School faculty.

CHAPTER V: DISCUSSION OF FINDINGS

Themes, Stages of Change, Organization of the Scheduling Committee and Training

This chapter analyzes the data and provides some observations and conclusions that may be of interest to schools researching restructuring through moving to a block schedule. Themes that transcend the change process for Shadle Park High School are noted in their developing process. The themes I have focused upon include the following:

1. Entering the change process

2. Emotional reactions to entering the change process

3. Physical change in process

4. Emotional change in process

Teachers could choose to stay and change, stay and not change, or leave the system. Training, support, and evaluation influenced teachers' reactions to the change process. The individuals involved in this study shared both professional and personal information about their experiences with the change process. As professional educators, they shared their accounts of their individual adjustments, problems, and joys. In some cases, they admitted to exhibiting behaviors not typical of their normal professional or personal conduct. The participants shared their experiences so other teachers in similar change processes may benefit. The experiences of the Shadle Park High School teachers paralleled some of the experiences of Kettle Falls teachers during my years as their principal while we adapted to the block schedule.

Themes

Emerging themes that I perceived throughout my observation process are illustrated through a diagram (see Figure 1).

DIAGRAM—FIGURE 1 WILL

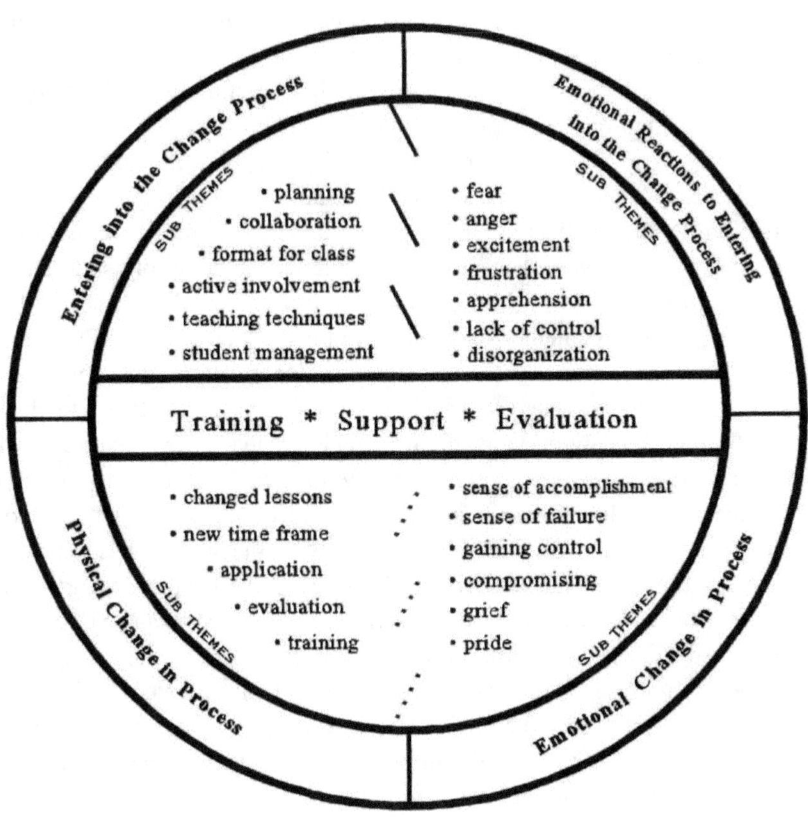

Figure 1.

Circle of Themes of Change, illustrated in Figure 1., demonstrates how themes and subthemes relate to one another.

The diagram consists of a circle divided into four sections. On each side of the upper part of the circle are indicators detailing two specific themes: "Entering the Change Process" and "Emotional Reactions to Entering the Change Process." The line with both smooth and jagged portions which separates these two upper areas symbolizes the inconsistency the people involved experienced as a result of change. The lower half of the circle denotes change in process on both a physical and an emotional level. The "Physical Change in Process" and the "Emotional Change in Process" themes and sub-themes are divided by jagged and dotted lines to indicate the difficulty, even impossibility, of separating them.

The first theme, "Entering the Change Process," includes several subthemes: planning teaching techniques, format for class, active involvement, student management, and collaboration. The second theme, "Emotional Reactions to Entering the Change Process," has the following subthemes: fear, apprehension, frustration, disorganization, lack of control, anger, and excitement. The third theme, "Physical Change in Process," has these sub-themes: changed lessons, new time frame, training, application, and evaluation. The fourth theme, "Emotional Change in Process," involves the following subthemes: compromising, gaining control, grief, pride, sense of failure, and sense of accomplishment. The middle band in the circle of themes labeled "Training, Support, and Evaluation" illustrates the means of easing teachers from the upper themes and subthemes to the lower themes and subthemes. Teachers who responded positively to change through training, receiving and giving support, and growing through the evaluation process accepted the opportunity to learn and make adjustments required by the schedule change. Their degree of learning and adjusting varied, depending upon their individual abilities to cope with the many levels of pain this change caused. The teachers experienced professional and personal growth in direct proportion to their own need for changes they wanted to make or that they were assigned as a result of the new schedule, and their own willingness to accommodate the changes they wanted to make or that they were assigned as a result of the new schedule. The four themes and their sub themes are an integral part of the analysis of the data and the terms arising throughout the following discussion. Current literature often addresses these themes and subthemes as integral to the change process and is cited specifically throughout the chapter.

Hord et al. (1987) developed as part of their Concerns-Based Adoption Model (CBAM) a portion labeled Stages of Concern (SoC) which is presented in Chapter II. Figure 1 relates to the two dimensions, self, and task. The stages within Hord et al.'s SoC include stage 1, information; stage 2, personal; and stage 3, management. The upper left area of figure 1, "Entering into the Change Process," relates to Hord et al.'s information stage. The remainder of figure 1 further develops the information stage and the management stage. This research focused on the initial year of implementation of the block schedule at Shadle Park High School; therefore, Hord and Hall's third dimension of impact is not pertinent to these findings.

The following information describes each theme and subtheme named in figure 1. Examples from Shadle Park High School teachers, citations from the literature review, and, in some cases, similarities I experienced with Kettle Falls teachers develop the themes and sub-themes.

Entering the Change Process

Many teachers at Shadle Park High School knew from early discussions in faculty meetings about adjustments to traditional teaching with block scheduling's longer time frame and from reports by teachers who made visitations to other schools with block schedules that change was an integral part of the movement to the long block of teaching time. Fine (1994) explained that teachers' comfort zones might be seriously challenged when the idea of change becomes a reality. Many teachers who thought they were ready for this change began having doubts about their ability to adjust successfully. Amy noted, "I used to be great in 50 minutes—really great. Then I became concerned, and I lacked confidence in what I would be like in 100 minutes."

During the summer prior to the implementation of the block schedule, Corina involved herself in planning lessons to the minute per class period. Corina stated, "I recall during the summer breaking down and crying with a friend and fellow teacher, not knowing what I would do because I had convinced myself that I could not do this." Fullan (1991) indicated that people involved in change often do not view the change in its full perspective and that people accept changes in a variety of degrees of acceptance. Some people adjust to change more readily than others. Many teachers indicated that they had to change in the areas of planning, teaching techniques, format for their classes, their own and their students' active involvement in the classes, the way they managed students, and their need for collaboration with both colleagues and students.

Several teachers at Kettle Falls High School dedicated very few hours to planning prior to implementing the block schedule. As their principal, I was aware of some confusion, frustration, and anger teachers experienced because they had underestimated the impact of impending change upon their teaching. The Kettle

Falls teachers had received a little training, but they responded positively—some were excited—because they received more training than they had received in the past and more than other teachers in the district at the time. Due to the financial constraints of the district, financial support was limited to paying for training. Once the school year was underway, teachers seemed as though they were on a fast track, hurling themselves into their work, with little time to take advantage of the option to visit other schools and work with other teachers in their subject areas who had experience in block teaching and planning. In retrospect, I wish I would have increased the training sessions for these teachers, especially prior to the inception of the new schedule. Their excited attitude about having more training than they had ever had before tended to cloud their real need for training.

The following facets of the themes, which I have illustrated in Figure 1, indicated some of the areas of change the Shadle Park High School teachers experienced. These areas include planning, teaching techniques, format for class, active involvement, student management, and collaboration.

<u>Planning</u>. Several teachers indicated that they had planned extensively during the summer to be ready for the first month or the first quarter of the school year. Amy noted that many teachers started the school year with the block schedule in excellent spirits, but around the beginning of October, tension seemed to be growing:

By the end of September, all their [teachers'] lesson plans had run out. Really, this literally happened . . . and the stress level was so high, it was coming out in odd ways. A few teachers would admit to being stressed. But many teachers would be in my office complaining about something an administrator did or something their department head did. Teachers who in the past never complained were complaining.

Planning seemed to be a key element in maintaining stability for many staff members, but once the school year was underway, a lack of time for adequate planning in this new block period seemed to cause stress for many teachers. Zaltman and Duncan (1977) noted that individuals and groups undergoing change were re-learning their duties. Teachers had to re-learn how to plan in new ways to accommodate the change in time segments. Shadle Park High School teachers had a 50-minute period on Mondays and two 100-minute periods on two of the four remaining days of the week. Two days per week, teachers did not have scheduled preparation time, and on those days, they taught three 100-minute blocks in a row.

A similar reaction to insufficient planning affected many Kettle Falls teachers. I detected reluctance on the part of many teachers to share their emotional concerns. As a staff, we met every week and committed to hearing each other make at least one statement each about how we were dealing with the block schedule. At first, comments were brief, but by October, teachers were more open about their planning problems, as well as other issues. When a teacher seemed in need of assistance, several other teachers were available—sometimes with similar problems—to listen, help, and share concerns. Approximately one-fourth of the teachers had preparation daily at the same time, which also provided them with more collegial sharing moments when they chose to get together.

The Kettle Falls teachers taught three 90-minute blocks per day and had a 90-minute preparation period each day. The regular daily planning time seemed, to some degree, to help offset the lack of training and prevented the depth of the stress the Shadle Park High School teachers felt when they ran out of summer-prepared lessons and materials. The Kettle Falls teachers still felt stressed and stretched in the face of changes the new schedule brought to them. Having 90 minutes daily helped provide a meaningful, productive period of time to prepare for classes and to work with some of their colleagues. I believe most Kettle Falls teachers grew more trusting and dependent upon one another as they worked through their concerns in regard to the changes they were experiencing. I also believe that a few teachers who were having serious problems adjusting simply kept to themselves their lack of success in making adjustments. Because the majority of the teachers expressed a positive attitude toward the change, they did not want to appear unable or unwilling to meet this challenge. They kept up the appearance of participating in the change process and found appropriate comments to share to prevent the discovery of their real experience.

<u>Teaching Techniques.</u> For some teachers, the move to the longer time frame meant that they had to make adjustments in their teaching techniques. Some teachers who lectured, for example, found the transition difficult. Tim indicated, "I was not just a lecturer, but an entertainer, moving students through vast amounts of information quickly." For Tim, the change was difficult. He had many years of successful experience in 50-minute periods. He realized that students could not give the same attention to him for 100 minutes, nor could he be as dynamic for 100 minutes as he was for 50 minutes. Darling-Hammond (1995) noted that teachers reinvent teaching and learning processes. Bridges (1991) pointed out that in order to change, teachers must give up the old ways of operating, grieving the loss of the old ways. Then they can begin to make the new

approaches to teaching part of their system of teaching, as well as part of themselves.

Corina described herself as a linear planner and generally a lecture-oriented presenter. With the change she explained, "A teacher next door was project-oriented, and I asked her for some ideas for activities. She, in turn, needed some concrete ideas to enrich her lessons. We found a way to help each other, which lifted my attitude further." Dooley (1992) noted that lecture as the basis for full-class instruction is changing to a more active, dynamic process.

Format for Class. Making adjustments in the format for classes did not seem to come easily for a number of teachers. Some teachers indicated that they were comfortable with students sitting for 50 minutes, listening to a lecture, taking notes, and then moving on to their next class. With 100 minutes, many teachers had to learn how to teach students using other ways of presenting material, such as student participation in small group learning activities in addition to lecture portions of the class. One teacher explained he was used to providing all of the instruction and that when the larger block of time kept happening every day, he had to develop ways to reformat his class. He noted that he ran out of energy and that his students could not seem to stay focused for a longer period. Kane (1994) noted the need to provide teachers time to learn new delivery methods, which may help teachers create more effective formats for class instruction.

Active Involvement. For teachers who have dominated class presentations, actively involving students in their own learning processes was difficult for these reasons: teachers' habits of always being the "sage on the stage" and the teacher's lack of confidence in students' abilities to present material clearly and thoroughly. Lois noted, "I fear that some teachers are not making the adjustment necessary to make the longer blocks of time work. They are overusing videos and teaching ineffectively—they just opt to fill time with anything to get through. I worry about the total school program and the loss of quality across several areas.

With more time in one class on a daily basis, many teachers need to be willing to engage their students in projects and assignments that extend beyond the classroom. English (1993) noted that school boundaries might include the community, as well as county services and agencies, such as libraries, hospitals, businesses, social services, and hospitals. Some teachers assisted their students in finding the relevance of class learning to their larger world.

Keith, as a special education teacher, stated, "Moving to the 100-minute periods was a smooth transition in my special program. We have to be flexible, to begin with. Our focus is directed toward getting our students into the real world, and this new time frame enhances our program. "

Whether teachers confined themselves to learning in the classroom or whether they extended their lessons into the community and the larger world focus, the active involvement of students became unavoidable in the larger time frame. Passive student participation, which included listening to lectures, taking notes and tests, and repeating these activities throughout a course, did not seem to work for some teachers and students in the longer time period. Tim noted, "Teachers had to rethink their approach to things and offer a variety of activities, appealing to students' various learning styles." Darling-Hammond (1995) noted the importance of reinventing teaching and applying different approaches in presenting information to students.

Those Kettle Falls teachers whose main delivery of information was lecturing struggled—some more than others—with the 90-minute block of time. Students in their classes became frustrated at times with these teachers, and they were vocal to their teachers and to me about being bored by full-period lectures. The complaining students added to these teachers' concerns and, at least in some cases, prompted teachers to work on actively involving students by varying their delivery methods. Regardless of the complaints, some teachers continually returned to their comfort zone of the lecture for long periods of time. A few teachers chose not to adjust teaching methods to the block time frame. The alternative—changing to new teaching methods—is more than just difficult. Changing may have been an admission that their previous years of experience were invalidated by a change that could be successful. In other words, a teacher may say inwardly or unconsciously, "If this is the way I should have been teaching all along, then my past 20+ years of teaching were done incorrectly. I can't accept that."

Student Management. Gaining the cooperation of students in the 100-minute period seemed to vary for teachers. Some teachers found the longer period pleasant and productive. One teacher noted that students interacted with one another more with in-depth practice over a longer period. She stated, "Students have not lost effective learning opportunities in the transition from the traditional schedule to the block schedule." One of the Kettle Falls vocational teachers developed a Community Resource Training Program (CRT) and placed students in businesses for one block per day. Each block was backed up to non-instructional time (before or after school or lunchtime), allowing students travel time from school to job sites and back to other classes as needed. Although this program was available in the traditional schedule, students were only assigned during the late afternoon period to avoid missing other classes. The block schedule opened the full day for CRT assignments. This program gained recognition in the community, students filled the quota allowed per year, and several students were on a waiting list.

Although students adapted quickly to some programs, such as CRT, change for them was not easy. Fullan (1991) noted that people who move from a familiar practice to a new practice might be confused about what they are giving up. Some students experienced frustration and confusion as teachers varied in their expectations of student behavior (Bridges, 1991). Students who had been used to passive participation found the role as active participants that their teachers expected of them unfamiliar, uncomfortable, and even unattainable for themselves. Bridges noted that confusion is a normal reaction for people involved in change. Some students who found this change uncomfortable or unattainable became behavior problems by acting out, refusing to cooperate with others, including the teachers, or they withdrew from participation.

When Kettle Falls High School began studying the block schedule, students had a role in the process. Prior to the selection of the specific type of block schedule, students had input through a series of meetings with the school counselor and me. We met with groups of 50 to 70 students for discussion and questioning sessions, where we illustrated several types of block schedules. We included student representatives on visitations to other schools using block schedules. As we developed the rough draft of the first schedule, we pre-registered our student body to see if the drafts met their selection needs. Based on student input, we made several adjustments to the master schedule.

Shadle Park High School did not involve students in the developmental or planning processes. Amy indicated that because teachers were responsible for making the schedule work and because teachers were in charge of the educational program, they needed to make the decisions, not the students. The size of the student body, 1,500 students, made meaningful involvement difficult as compared to Kettle Falls' 300 students. Because I did not interview students, I made no judgments about involving students in planning. I enjoyed working with the Kettle Falls students, however, and I felt the students made positive suggestions that enhanced the developmental process. I must admit that because we involved students in the process, they were vocal about their concerns both to teachers and to me. Many students voiced complaints when they felt lectures were too long, activities required too much of their time or attention, teachers were asking too much of them, or any other problem that they could relate to the schedule change.

Teachers, the counselor, and I spent time working with students who found fault with the new system. In some cases, the complaints were a result of students' own lack of receptiveness to change. Some teachers did not appreciate the complaints from students. I believe, however, that students' complaints contributed to the reduction of long lectures and the increase in varied learning activities. Some students preferred lecture-based instruction. When these students were not expected to speak out, work in a team or groups, or make presentations, classes were easier, safer, consistent, and comfortable for them. Some of these students accused teachers who used to lecture all period of not doing their jobs or of making students do the teaching.

<u>Collaboration</u>. Many teachers accepted roles in researching and implementing the block schedule. Derrington (1988) notes that principals serve their teachers best by empowering teachers to take on leadership roles throughout the change process. Encouraging teachers to collaborate with one another eased the transition. Berry (1995) contended that teachers who work as part of professional and collegial teams might find change easier to implement than teachers who are not used to team participation. Some teachers were not used to collegial teamwork and discovered that the change was more difficult due to their own lack of cooperation with other teachers. Amy noted, "We included time for teachers to meet in their departments so they could collaborate with one another frequently." With a change to the longer periods, some teachers sought out colleagues to discuss their professional and personal concerns during the transition process. Majchrzak (1984) noted the need for clear and timely communication among stakeholders from the beginning and throughout the change process. Derrington (1988) indicated that teachers need to become partners whose ideas are valued and shared in order to embrace change.

At Kettle Falls, teachers communicated with one another at weekly teachers' meetings. Every teacher made the commitment to make at least one statement about how he or she was experiencing the block schedule. Some teachers shared with me that they were conversing in the teachers' room more frequently about professional concerns and less frequently about noneducation matters than they had been aware of in the past. Comments at the weekly teachers' meetings often related to the help one teacher had received from another teacher in lesson planning, the use of energizing activities, or how to improve in some areas of time management.

Teachers seemed to work more collaboratively than they had in the past. Having a common preparation period with one-fourth of the staff increased collaboration. Teachers were limited to the same group, however, due to a consistent daily schedule. Kettle Falls teachers needed even more collaborative time with one another. The process did not provide them with departmental and collegial interactions as well as it could have. We realized how important communication was to the teachers. A few teachers simply did not adapt to the block schedule with any consistency, and more preparation, collegial time, and guidance may have helped them. The Shadle Park High School collaborative period prior to classes each morning was a consistent daily way to bring teachers together.

Emotional Reaction to Entering the Change Process

The Shadle Park High School teachers voted to accept the block schedule, but the vote was not unanimous. Some teachers did not want this change, and for some teachers, the change seemed forced upon them. Roger stated, "Change was forced upon us. I went from being a well-respected teacher to being a troublemaker because I opposed the switch." Many teachers who voted for the block schedule had second thoughts after their summer lesson plans, and other class preparations were used up by October or November. Returning to the traditional schedule during the school year was not an option. Fullan and Miles (1992) noted that obstacles to change include a lack of time for planning and preparing new ways to teach.

Some of the areas of emotional reactions that teachers experienced include fear, apprehension, frustration, disorganization, lack of control, anger, and excitement. Exploring these areas in relation to the Shadle Park High School change to a block schedule brings a focus on understanding the change experience itself.

<u>Fear.</u> Some teachers experienced fear. Corina shared her fear as she approached her first day in the block schedule, "Before the first day, I had trouble sleeping, and when school actually started, my trauma worsened. I felt I needed more training and more time to observe other teachers. I felt alone and unprepared." Fullan (1991) indicated that losing track of the emotional impact teachers experience may reduce the success of positive change in education.

Having a safe environment encouraged teachers to take risks at both Shadle Park High School and Kettle Falls High School. If teachers fear losing their positions or quality evaluations because they try new techniques and risk failing, they may not attempt an unsafe zone. John stated, "Administrators must provide a safe environment for teachers in order for them to be able to take risks and share their errors as well as their successes."

Encouraging teachers to communicate openly at teachers' meetings seemed to help Kettle Falls teachers learn to trust one another. Frequent, open opportunities to share successes and failures alleviated some of the fear change often generates. Bolman and Deal (1984) noted that when people cannot express their individual concerns and successes, organizations become inefficient. Communication was an essential factor for teachers to experience success.

Apprehension. Many teachers were apprehensive about whether their colleagues would be able to bring about the change together, along with their individual concerns about their own performances. Keith stated, "It's been really amazing to me. I never thought I would see the positive approach and that people really seemed to buy into it."

Ann indicated her apprehension as she read the results of the staff vote to move to this schedule. she stated, "I began to realize I was going to have to change, and I was unsure of how successful I would be in making that change." Ann had been involved in the development process, the scheduling committee, and training. She had been dedicated to the inception of this schedule, and as she saw the concrete evidence that the change was going to happen (the posted results of the teachers' vote on the block schedule), she experienced the realization that this was going to make a major change in her own professional career. Cherniss (1995) noted that people who are expected to change as a result of an organization's restructuring process might lose their own sense of competence.

Frustration. The feelings of frustration that some teachers experienced seemed to move in and out of their teaching day on a regular basis. Lois noted that some teachers who were frustrated became ineffective at times:

Some teachers run out of ideas. They have trouble adjusting to the longer time frame, and they can't figure out how to keep their students interested in their lessons. They can see students with blank stares hoping the bell will ring."

Sarason (1990) and Hargreaves (1994) noted that teachers with the desire to change have a greater possibility of achieving change, but having a full teaching load while at the same time trying to make major changes can be frustrating for them.

Some of the Kettle Falls teachers indicated their frustration to me, as well as to their colleagues. I appreciated their open dialogues about their frustrations because by discussing their concerns, they often found colleagues with similar feelings and some with suggestions that might lead to solutions. I now see the need for more organized group training and more individual training and assistance for frustrated teachers. My own lack of knowledge about the repercussions of changing to the block schedule, and about change itself, limited my ability to serve teachers more immediately and effectively.

<u>Disorganization</u>. In the early stages of developing the format for the block schedule, Amy noted, "We seemed to spin our wheels in our lack of focus. A few committee members wanted to look at one schedule model only while others wanted to review several block options."

Mark stated, "The people on the committee were not able to direct their energy toward a plan on which they could agree." Liebeman, Darling-Hammond, and Zucherman (1991) pointed out that when a school system decides to change in a major way, conflict may develop as a normal part of the process. In time, the committee membership changed, and eventually, the members were able to present a few options on which the staff could vote.

The Kettle Falls teachers looked at several options and seemed to move toward their final choice due to an organized scheduling committee. The members were selected by the full teaching staff as the group of individuals they felt would best represent them. No one was asked to volunteer, nor was anyone assigned without a willingness to serve. During the first few months, all of us felt somewhat unorganized in many ways. But the process seemed to give the committee members a sense of confidence in that they represented a group that respected their participation on its behalf.

<u>Anger</u>. As the Shadle Park High School scheduling committee grappled with their lack of focus, the membership changed. Amy explained, "Some members of the committee quit when the AB block schedule became the focus of the majority of the group." A few members of the committee did not, according to Amy, want a change of any kind. Some members had a different type of schedule in mind.

Amy indicated that some members quit out of anger and feelings of being alienated from the group.

The voting process brought out anger in some teachers. Amy noted, "People were accusing each other of trying to undermine the governance process. It was very, very uncomfortable."

Teachers complained more about some of their colleagues and became so angry with one another that they argued openly at meetings. Amy indicated that she was afraid that some staff members would blow up at one another or at John and her [administrators].

<u>Excitement</u>. The energy of many teachers was high when the school opened in September. Teachers who had planned well during the summer and teachers in areas that easily adapted to longer blocks of time were excited as school began and while their plans lasted. For some teachers, that excitement became negative when they had used up their plans. Fine (1994) indicated that teachers might appear ready for change, but when their comfort zones are seriously challenged, they may become unsure or unwilling to accept change.

As the year progressed, some teachers became excited about their ability to adapt and grow professionally. Lois, Corina, and Ann shared their feelings of excitement at being able to learn and apply new techniques successfully after having over 20 years of each non-traditional teaching methodology. They also shared the difficulties they faced in the challenge of changing. I was aware of the tremendous effort of the Kettle Falls High School teachers, who seemed to adapt easily to change. These teachers may have made the process look easy, but they worked hard for their achievements. I recall assisting one lecture-based teacher several times in one week while he tried to use small group instruction in one of his classes. He seemed to struggle, blaming himself for his lack of ability to keep all students on task in his new venture. He needed assurances that he was doing well. When he realized that the students also had to learn how to function differently in this setting, he concentrated on their roles as participants and helped them adjust. Compared to his first try, his subsequent group lessons were noticeably improved. This excellent, lecture-based teacher was becoming competent in another delivery system, but not without effort, planning, and pain.

Training, Support, and Evaluation

These three areas provided many teachers with the tools to adjust to the block schedule. John indicated, "We had a lot of training." John explained that departments wrote their own proposals, identified their needs, and designed their own training during the year prior to going to this schedule. Roscoe and Whitford (1991) noted that teachers expressed positive experiences when they had administrative support and meaningful participation in the change process. Administrators were supportive in dealing with operational needs. Teachers expressed positive experiences when they had supportive administration, a role in decision making, and colleagues actively and willingly participating in change in a student-centered environment.

At Kettle Falls, during the first month of the block schedule implementation, our staff and I were amazed at the number of minor occurrences that arose due to the block schedule. The lunch schedule, library schedules, bus schedules, and many activities were a few of the areas affected. Although we had foreseen a few of these issues, we had to make adjustments to avoid losing more time out of one period than out of another due to assemblies, school activities, and other school functions. As a staff, we agreed to examine our individual programs and how they may be influenced by the new time frame with the goal of catching and correcting problems in advance.

Physical Change in Process

Once the school year started, teachers and students were part of the new schedule every day, attempting to adjust as the educational program was in process. The summer training and planning became part of the daily routine. Teachers were involved in change which I have examined in each of the following areas: changed lessons, a new time frame, training, application, and evaluation.

Changed Lessons. With the larger block of time, most teachers found that they needed to make adjustments in their lesson planning. Mark stated, "It forces a teacher to be more prepared for lessons, planning all parts of the time frame." A teacher who had experienced success as a lecturer in the 50-minute period did not change his delivery method for some time. His students could not tolerate him day after day of his lecturing, and several students complained to me about having to sit through his constant talking with no breaks for 100 minutes. During weekly teachers' meetings, I brought up the students' concerns generally with classes where lecturing was taking place throughout the period and asked teachers to share energizers and activities involving students that they use in their classes. Teachers openly shared their ideas, and fortunately, lecturing teachers accepted their ideas and supported them in how to carry out their ideas. I also talked with the lecturing teachers privately when possible about the student complaints —and when the complaints began subsiding because these teachers were limiting their lecture time, I shared that with them and congratulated them on making this change in the delivery of their lessons. We all could see that change needed to happen, and change is definitely not easy. In fact, for some teachers, change was painful.

Students helped make change possible for teachers who found that as they spent more time focusing on how students would receive and benefit from their lessons, they worried less about their own problems. The key to changing successfully was to focus on the students and their learning styles and, as one teacher stated, "Let's quit feeling sorry for ourselves and make this happen for our students in the most effective way possible."

Training. John explained that the teachers could design and develop their own training to make it meet their specific needs. Administration made it a priority to find available inservice providers to support the training teachers wanted. Training could also include inservice at other schools or at other sites, visitations to schools, and bringing other teachers to work with individuals and departments.

Amy explained, "Teachers have had training, but the self-training they have done for themselves on their own has been essential." Teachers who apply and reapply training ideas discuss their progress with colleagues and continue challenging themselves to grow to find success in the block schedule.

John and Amy researched inservices in several ways. They called other districts that were using block schedules for recommendations for inservice providers that offered presentations specifically related to teaching in a block schedule. Some recommendations proved helpful, but other recommendations, after follow-up calls to teachers in districts where the training sessions were given, gave a teacher-centered recommendation that was not always positive. By checking, researching, and then hiring the provider most highly recommended, John and Amy brought mostly teacher training sessions that the teachers felt were good. Kane (1994) noted the importance of providing quality training. Without quality training, many teachers may be unable to change their teaching styles.

According to Kane, training may also alleviate anxiety in teachers and students as teachers apply what they learned through training.

Prior to the inception of the block schedule, the only training the Kettle Falls teachers received to help with teaching and delivery of information was on cooperative learning. They also could visit teachers in their subject areas in other schools, but very few teachers did this. During the planning year, teachers did not think about this seriously, and once the initial year of the block schedule was underway, they were caught up in the process and felt unable to leave—perhaps too rushed to take time away from their classes. As their principal, I wish I had realized how important additional training was for many of the teachers and that I had provided teachers with more training, more visitations to their teachers in their teaching areas, and more time to learn how to deliver information in various areas.

Application. When Shadle Park High School applied the new schedule to their system, the teachers responded in a multitude of ways. The change that took place was much more than an adjusted bell schedule.

Amy noted after the first year had ended, "Schools that make this change should spend the first year taking care of the teachers. Provide time for them to work with one another in their departments, and do not use their hesitancy in trying new ways to teach as a negative factor in their teaching evaluations. There is no way we could have anticipated just how much this change could affect teachers professionally and personally.

Glickman (1993) indicated the importance of scheduling time for teachers to communicate with one another. Fullan and Miles (1992) noted that colleagues need more time to communicate with one another about their lesson plans and teaching techniques.

Jerry noted, "If teachers are doing this right, there will be no opportunity to slack off." Because teachers needed to change some of their ways of performing their teaching duties, they needed time to work with colleagues, share ideas, and practice assisting one another in applying this scheduling system. Senge (1990) indicated the need to see ourselves as connected to a common experience, not isolated from one another.

Evaluation. In any change, an evaluation process assists in guiding the people involved toward improvements. Evaluation that opens growth opportunities to individuals and groups of colleagues offers an invitation to take risks and try new techniques in the planning and delivery of lessons. But when the evaluation process instills fear, anger, or frustration with a lack of growth potential, the person attempting change will find the process inhibiting.

John stated, "An administrator who follows the typical evaluation approach of looking for problems in a teacher's performance and who pounces on each infraction with the goal of improving a teacher's performance and, at the same time, making sure that teacher knows who's boss, is going to add stress, anxiety, and fear—not improved performance. With all the changes teachers face in moving to a block schedule, the typical "I'm the boss" attitude is only going to harm the teacher. Taking risks to make plans that work in the new time frame needs to be encouraged and respected, not punished."

The evaluation process caused frustrations to the surface for several Kettle Falls teachers. The more experienced teachers tended to worry more about their formal evaluations than newer teachers, but I was aware that this was a sensitive issue with the staff. Regardless of the care I took in the evaluation process, a few teachers expressed their fears that their evaluations would reflect poor performance due to their attempts at new techniques that may not have worked out as well as they thought they should have worked—or attempts that outright failed.

Teachers need to be free from the fear of failure in order to try new approaches to teaching. As principal, I did not want to hinder enthusiasm while helping teachers improve their teaching. I also experienced frustrations in trying to balance their successes and their areas of growth. The completed form itself is of immense importance to some teachers. If teachers have to risk a poor evaluation after having years of truly outstanding evaluations, they hesitate to attempt change. The dilemma for them, however, is that if they do not change, they may flounder terribly in the longer block of time, and their evaluations will reflect that as well. The principal's role needs to be supportive and honest. As principal, I needed to step into each teacher's role and see her or his teaching successes and areas of concern that had to be improved for students' sake. I found that I needed to dramatically increase the number of visits with teachers, not only in their classes but also one-on-one, to learn about their concerns and to help them find solutions to their teaching problems.

Patterson, Purkey, and Parker (1986) noted that the principal needs to serve as a teacher, continually sharing with teachers the direction the school district is going and the ways to reach the goals and objectives. By valuing teachers, positive administrators establish trust. With a trusting relationship, growth is possible.

Emotional Change in Process

The teachers participating in the study often experienced the gamut of emotions that any group of people or individuals experience when confronted with a major change in their professional career. Some teachers felt they had to compromise their professional security to step into new methods of teaching. Gaining control of the change situation was not as easy for some teachers as for others. Grief and pride touched some teachers at different times and to varying degrees. The sense of failure was integrated with a sense of accomplishment as some lessons fell flat with either students or the teacher, and some lessons soared with excellence for both students and teacher. The following sections present illustrations of how teachers responded to these several emotions: compromising, gaining control, grief, pride, a sense of failure, and a sense of accomplishment.

Compromising. According to Ann and Lois, secondary teachers generally seem to place more emphasis on teaching content than they place on individual student learning. Lois noted the 100-minute period might become long when the students and the teacher are not in a joint, positive learning process. Lois commented that teachers who are content-driven need to compromise with their comfort mode of teacher-directed delivery and make contact with each student.

Ann indicated, "The focus for high school teachers here is now moving toward students as their first responsibility, and the subject or material as the second. We are really here for students, so it's a great thing." Compromise may guide teachers through the change process as they negotiate with themselves to change the known for the unknown. Miles and Huberman (1984) noted that people might participate in the practice of change before the change is accepted into their own belief systems.

Gaining Control. Both teachers and students experienced less stress and more control of their school day with the block schedule. From the students' perspective, meeting the needs of three classes per day was easier to deal with in several ways, even though the time frame was longer. Having fewer teachers per day made a major difference for students. For teachers, the same was true: having three classes of students (80 to 90 students per day) offered teachers the real possibility of relating to individual students daily, compared to having 180 students per day. For both students and teachers, stress levels were low or eliminated, and feeling personally in control of the school day for individuals was a positive result.

Grief and Failure. Teachers experienced the emotions of grief and failure. Giving up teaching the material they had taught in a certain way for years had to change. This created uncertainty, and loss of confidence in front of students and in themselves when they changed methods and materials. It was as though a major part of their successful teaching career was dying, and grieving this failure happened deeply to many teachers in regard to major portions of their years of teaching.

A Sense of Failure and Pride. At the outset of moving to the long blocks, many teachers felt lost in the process and personally insecure when students did not respond as the teachers had planned. Teachers made many attempts to make lessons successful with the hope of excellence, only to find they came up short many more times than they expected. Their sense of failure haunted them. However, as they continued exploring new methods of presenting material through a variety of activities that they learned from colleagues and from their own research and trials, a sense of pride began to develop that, over time, lifted their spirits and provided feelings of success.

whwhwhwhwhwhwhwhwhwhwhwhwhwhwhwhwhwhwhwhwhwhwhwhwh

What Happened?

Commencement Speech by the Principal

Your Town High School in U.S., America

For some of you, high school was great. You excelled in academics, sports, music, and other social involvement, and I congratulate you on your achievements. Maybe you sang in the choir, played in the band, or worked in the library or cafeteria. Perhaps you rebuilt engines or wrote for the school newspaper. Maybe you were lucky just to get to school on time, or a little late, or had frequent absences due to problems at home. I congratulate every one of you for your talents and achievements and on your graduation today.

Statistics verify that most graduates had difficult times during these high school years. Popularity may or may not have been attained, friendships may have been few, or not close—or not at all. Bullying was often expected—daily or hourly. Unfortunately, some students were lonely, sad, and unable to fit in or achieve what they hoped for. And—unable or unwilling to ask for help. Or maybe someone asked for help, but nothing happened, and no help came. The "popular" kids were just as messed up as the ignored or rejected ones. Their thoughts: "What if I don't get elected to ____? or "chosen for___?" So many "What ifs" and "I'll just die if I don't make it." I am also sure that many students made it through high school happy and well adjusted.

When I was in high school, I was one of the "out crowd." Working at home doing chores, taking care of my baby sister, living in an abusive situation, working a job. When I expressed an interest in going to college, the counselor told me that was not going to happen and that I would never make it. He wouldn't even approve of my taking Algebra 2. "You don't need it," the counselor said to me. "You'll probably marry a miner and have a bunch of kids. College isn't for kids like you."

My message to every one of you today: Believe in yourself. Look for opportunities. Take a chance—a leap of faith. Many years from now, you may amaze yourself as you review your achievements. Do not let your teenage years define your future.

You don't know yet just how smart you are or how gifted you are in so many possible areas. Think you can succeed, and you will. Step out there and do the right things, go places, and speak up for yourself. You have to be your own cheerleader now. If one thing doesn't work, try another. Listen, pay attention, and look for opportunities. Learn what an opportunity requires; prepare, then apply. If the first time doesn't work, try again—and again. Set-backs happen, but keep trying. Practice does make a difference. If, at your age, I had only listened to well-meaning people telling me what I couldn't do, I would have missed out not only on my best achievements but also on being the one who encouraged other people, like all of you, to attain their goals.

This is your chance, your achievement, your life. I know you can succeed if you believe in yourself—and you make it happen. You can't depend on someone else to do this for you. I believe you can succeed, one small—OR BIG— step at a time. You believe it. It's your time.

It is also your time to encourage your students. Tell them they can succeed. Build them up. Help them feel safe in school, connected to other students, and have a meaningful connection to school.

A High School Administrator

What could have happened? This high school's teachers and administrators could have been more aware of ways to lessen the negative impact students were experiencing. Instead of simply being aware that bullying was happening, there could have been a plan to stop it and a way for students to feel safe reporting it. A major way to alleviate negativity would have been to research other ways to schedule courses. The block schedule alleviates disciplinary problems by limiting the number of passing times each day, a time when inappropriate behavior waves through every hallway and can negatively impact a major part of any student body.

What did happen? These students graduated, and with that diploma in hand, they stand an excellent chance of getting employment and/or furthering their training and education. Unfortunately, the 32% of the class who did not graduate and either dropped out or were expelled during their time in this school face an uncertain future. Some will be unemployed. Some already have or will face jail time, and of these former students, at least 12% will go to prison. Being homeless, unemployed, and mental illness may also be a part of the future for several of them.

We can make life better for students in our nation by changing the way we are doing public school education. With a schedule that accommodates the learning styles of students, a teaching staff that is better prepared to accommodate students' learning styles, and a system that wants to keep students in school and complete school successfully, we can reduce homelessness, unemployment, crime, mental illness, poverty, and send our young graduates from school to have a much better life. Stopping isolation and expulsion as punishments does not mean that students are not held accountable. Schools need to hold them accountable within the system, not kick them out. Many schools are doing this successfully. We can learn from each other and support our students. A caring, well-organized elementary school is the foundation for students to find their way through high school. Ending isolation consequences—suspensions and expulsions—will go a long way toward helping students be successful. Together, we can do this.

whwhwhwhwhwhwhwhwhwhwhwhwhwhwhwhwhwhwhwhwhwhwhwhwhwhwhwhwh

Initial Stages of Change

The initial stages of change for Shadle Park High School began with trying to select a scheduling committee. The following sections describe the initial stages in this subheading: "Controversy in Organizing the Scheduling Committee," "Committee Member Selection," Volunteer Members," Educating the Committee Members," and "The Voting Process."

Controversy in Organizing the Scheduling Committee

The scheduling committee experienced controversy from the beginning of its formation. The members of the committee included teachers who wanted one specific kind of schedule, those who had no real preference for any format, and members who did not want a block schedule at all. The committee, as a result of its lack of focus, had difficulty making decisions, and it struggled to finally come up with one recommendation for a specific block schedule. Webb (1994) stressed that, for real change to occur, there needed to be an overall feeling of support. This committee did not seem to be focused or clear about a common vision for their school. Hansen and Liftin (1991) pointed out that if a school is not interested in or ready to create change, that change may be unworkable. The selection of the committee members is instrumental in getting the change process off to a smooth start.

As Kettle Falls High School principal, I recall my own confusion when some teachers told me privately their fears of a few senior teachers essentially taking over the process to keep the block schedule change from happening. These fearful teachers, however, would not express their concerns openly at staff meetings. I made it a point to ask all the teachers in our meetings to consider ways to select committee members that they felt represented and respected them and that they believed would not get caught up in their own agendas but would work to improve education as the primary goal of this committee.

Committee Member Selection

Having committed members who truly represent their teachers creates a strong potential that the teachers will respect the conclusions all of the teachers will respect. Fernandez (1993) noted that a shared vision of what the change is going to be is an essential ingredient for success. Because there are many scheduling formats to consider, having the teachers be open to many ideas is essential for results that fit the district. To assure openness, the teachers and I agreed that the larger body makes recommendations for the committee membership and that volunteering be avoided. Their recommendations should reflect individuals whom they believe will work with others, contribute to the group, represent the entire group, and provide skills that help develop a functioning, productive committee. The change process creates confusion and unrest among participants. Zaltman and Duncan (1977) described the process as re-learning ways of working together with respect for one another and for the process.

Shadle Park High School's scheduling committee could not reach an agreement among themselves, and, as a result, some members quit before the schedule was developed. Hargreaves (1994) and Sarason (1990) noted that teachers do not have the same level of interest in any given change process, and this may contribute to the individual frustration teachers experience when dealing with change. Any school or organization involved in developing a committee to guide schedule adoption needs to give serious consideration to how the membership of this committee will be decided.

I do not have the perfect solution, but I advise considering having the whole body select what they consider to be their ideal committee. At Kettle Falls High School, this method seemed to facilitate the teachers' acceptance of the committee. While making their choices, the Kettle Falls High School faculty focused on people whom they believed would work well together, contribute a variety of skills essential to a representative committee, and stay with the group to provide continuity for the duration, if possible. Newmann (1993) described the importance of outlining a plan or a process that fits the school and community— a student-centered plan. The committee is a factor in bringing a plan to the larger group, and, as such, its members need to have the larger issues of school restructuring for improving the education of students as their goal.

Volunteer Members

Members of committees in general often volunteer to serve. Volunteers may come to the group with preset ideas or even demands of their individual expectations. Using only volunteers as the way to develop a committee to investigate and plan a block schedule is not a wise course of action. Ford (1991) indicated that for some teachers, frustration due to the expectations of change might become unbearable. The person who volunteers to serve on the committee may be there to block change at all costs. Fullan noted that the pain, loss, and confusion of some people involved in change might lead them to actions they would not consider under other circumstances.

The Kettle Falls High School teachers considered who would serve on their scheduling committee in a manner that gave all teachers input in the process. The faculty as a whole-body decided that each teacher would submit a list of six teachers whom each person believed would best represent the teachers' concerns and work together effectively. Their choices of committee members would get along with one another and bring about results the full staff would respect. In addition, all scheduling meetings were open to other teachers who wanted to sit in. Non-committee members could contribute ideas, but they could not dominate the discussion. That decision helped the initial organization process. By a concerted effort to bring people together who will work together and whom the teachers believe will best represent the group, the chances of the committee recommending a course of action acceptable to the others involved would be greater. Marris (1974) indicated the importance of the total involvement of those affected by decisions leading to change.

Educating the Committee

Educating scheduling committee members and other teachers by sending them to observe other schools involved with block scheduling seemed to be an excellent way to help teachers see how the schedule works. Teachers then had the opportunity to find out both positive and negative information about the schedule from colleagues in their own subject areas. Marris (1974) noted that knowledge might reduce fear and apprehension. Because the change process has both personal and professional consequences for participants, the educational part prior to the implementation of the schedule of choice will provide for a smoother transition from the former schedule to the new one.

Schon (1971) stressed the difficulty of confronting too much change at once. As a member of the scheduling committee, I gained much more than education. I felt I gained a great deal of information about how the teachers with whom I traveled both to and from the other districts we visited felt about the impending changes. Our conversations in the van traveling to and from visited sites provided me with rich insights into their feelings and the feelings of other staff members in an informal, non-threatening atmosphere. Each return trip was filled with comments that compared and contrasted our vision and our goals with what teachers had observed. Majchrzak (1984) noted, "Timely communication is essential in the change process." I appreciated the opportunity to share these visitations, travel time, and the resulting depth of communication I experienced with fellow committee members. I was relearning how to communicate with my staff.

I found it interesting that the counselors at Shadle Park High School, in their search for ways to serve their at-risk students, became interested in the block schedule. The counselors traveled to several schools on a mission to find solutions to dealing with students displaying behavior and emotional problems. By opening their minds to possibilities, they brought additional ideas to Shadle Park High School in an area that they had not targeted in their search for solutions to at-risk student education. Counselors learned that schools using block schedules found that the schedule itself was contributing to helping at-risk students (Bottoms & Profession, 1991, Blank & Scaglione, 1992). Contributions toward moving in a new direction will come from many sources.

The conflict in the voting process itself at Shadle Park High School indicated that the lack of agreement prompted some teachers to go to interesting lengths to keep change from occurring. Ford (1995) and Sarason (1983) indicated that change is met with strong opposition and restriction for many participants. Planning in advance how the voting will take place can reduce the anxiety of change. The administrators, with the support of the district, provided funding for training teachers to teach in the block schedule. Roscoe and Whitford (1991) noted positive results in change situations with a supportive administration. Providing funding and decision-making to teachers to develop training demonstrated a trusting relationship between the administration and the teachers. By taking advantage of the summer to set up training sessions, teachers were able to plan several weeks of lessons, learn how to use teaching techniques they had not used before, and get firsthand information from other teachers who had experience in block periods.

Giving teachers the opportunity to develop their own training contributed to the success of several teachers. Learning how to cope with change eased the transition from one time frame to another. Teachers not only had to learn new delivery systems and ways to guide students in the longer time frame, but they also had to learn how to teach students new roles in their classrooms. Fine (1994) indicated that teachers whose comfort zones are challenged might find changing very difficult. Shadle Park High School made the transition possible through the previous fall training, the summer training, and the ongoing training during the school year.

The Kettle Falls teachers had less training than the Shadle Park High School teachers, and as their principal, I used our limited staff development funds to meet their needs as they had designated. Funding, however, was very limited in our district, and I do not believe we had enough training to begin the year with confidence. The teachers, due to limited funding, did not have the opportunity to gain as much professional training as I would have liked them to have prior to applying the block schedule. I commend Shadle Park High School on its training program. Districts seeking to adopt a block schedule need to plan a significant staff development program prior to moving to this schedule (Dooley, 1992). Providing relevant training may be difficult to do. Shadle Park High School had teachers organize the training they wanted, but they still found that some of the training was not relevant in some areas. The time spent seeking our effective training is an important investment of time and money to ensure quality training.

When the school opened, some of the teachers who had planned lessons all summer for the 100-minute blocks were excited and thrilled with their lessons and classes, yet others had difficulty making the changes they planned. Some teachers found that getting students to move to a more student-centered learning situation did not flow smoothly. Some teachers who had not planned well were adjusting nicely, yet others were doing poorly. Cherniss (1995) noted that some individuals lose their sense of competence as a result of change. Fine (1994) noted that continual use of familiar ways of teaching was more comfortable for teachers struggling with changing their years of practice. The training helped many teachers, and the subject areas contributed to the ease with which some teachers were able to change. For example, some teachers of vocational courses, physical education classes, and special education classes had little difficulty in the transition. For some of these teachers, planning became easier. Teachers who used lecture as their main delivery style tended to have problems incorporating hands-on activities and student-directed activities. Slavin (1990) indicated that students need a variety of teaching styles to accommodate their varied learning styles in order to accomplish their many learning needs. Even though some teachers' comfort levels were challenged, they may have slipped back into familiar methods that were ineffective in the block schedule.

A few experienced teachers at Kettle Falls seemed reluctant to participate in training, but they did so because all of the teachers were involved together for some of the training sessions. Many of these teachers asked for more training following the implementation of the block schedule. Schon (1971) indicated that the change process was overwhelming at first, and Marris (1974) noted that anxiety and struggle were part of real change. I was aware of teachers comparing concerns with one another and individually with me or another colleague, in small groups, and at teachers' meetings, expressing specific training needs. They used one another as a lifeline to survive in the midst of change. I assisted lecture-based teachers with small group instruction during class periods throughout the first and second years of the block schedule. One teacher, in particular, was experiencing frustration, yet with each renewed attempt, her skills in guiding students and completing the group exercise improved. After not having worked with her for a two-month period, I asked her how the group work was going. She admitted that she had not tried consistently since I had assisted her last. We agreed to renew our efforts, and after another round of assistance, her lesson plans reflected her continued effort on a periodic basis to provide small group instruction. My reflection on this experience brought to light that excellent teachers who are trying to change need assistance and encouragement from time to time to keep involved in the change process. The familiar ways tend to come back into practice easily and often (Bridges, 1991).

Training is helpful, but it is not the total answer for a smooth transition for everyone. During the initial year of change, advanced preparation is essential. Neimeyer (1992) supported training prior to actual restructuring. As Shadle Park High School teachers discovered, however, they had not prepared enough to take them through the school year. Some teachers had prepared through the first quarter and some through the first month. Sarason (1990) and Hargreaves (1994) noted that frustration levels were high for teachers trying to change while teaching a full schedule. When teachers ran out of lesson plans, some of them panicked; others were doing fine, depending on the subject areas and their own adaptability to change. Hargreaves noted that panic happens when time is limited, teaching obligations continue as in the past, and new expectations crowd in on teachers. Frustration, fear, and anxiety arose for teachers as a result of perceived change and implemented change.

Teachers in the Change Process

Those teachers who had to give up their traditional ways of teaching experienced more difficulty in the transition. Having success in relearning teaching skills depends on a person's willingness to accept change. The grieving process of giving up the familiar and the successful methods in exchange for the new, uncomfortable methods contributed to their insecurity, frustration, and fear. Change of this nature is deeply emotional for participants. Teachers questioned their own abilities to be effective educators. If teachers are aware that change is difficult and that fear and frustration are normal in this situation, they also need to know that the pain does not go away, but it makes working through it somewhat easier to accept.

A Kettle Falls teacher expressed his frustration to me. He stated, "As much as I try, the old ways keep coming back, and I feel angry that I can't keep doing what I have always done. It makes me feel like a failure." Many teachers feel deep emotional stress, and as I observed Shadle Park High School teachers, I more fully understood his pain and frustration. By sliding back into old ways that the teacher knows are no longer acceptable, the teacher experienced a loss of self-confidence and a loss of self-trust in his abilities to continue in his profession. Some teachers cannot overcome the pain, frustration, and stress change creates.

Finding ways to help teachers see the personal and professional individual benefits is an important way to enable teachers to open their minds to change. Some teachers expressed their reaffirmation as professional educators. Being able to adjust to new teaching techniques was professionally and personally exciting for them. Bridger (1991) explained that people who embrace change are able to give up their old ways of functioning. By providing collaborative time for teachers to relate to one another, the teachers experiencing success were able to energize those teachers who were struggling. Change may take place in practice before people accept change in their belief systems. When I became aware of Kettle Falls teachers helping one another, working departmentally or across curricular areas in support of one another, I made a point of taking an active interest in their collaboration. I complimented their efforts and served them as requested to observe, assist in lessons, and discuss outcomes as appropriate. As their principal, I felt the need to be available to them when they needed me. In retrospect, I often served them at their request. Had I been more knowledgeable about change, its consequences, and how this major change can influence teachers' lives, I could have served them more effectively and timely, easing the process, especially for the few teachers who struggled the most.

Relationship Between Teachers and Students in the Change Process

Several teachers indicated that the change to the longer blocks of time created more opportunities for teachers to build positive relationships. Longer blocks of time may have provided teachers and students with quality time for learning and building better rapport. Teachers met with fewer each day and in groups for longer periods of time. Some teachers were already comfortable with varying class activities, hands-on learning activities, and entrusting students with responsibilities for their learning. Other teachers fought the change, and as a result, they were unhappy, confused, and frustrated—sometimes acting out of their own self-interest, spending their energy in ways that helped them survive.

Students respond positively to teachers who provide meaningful involvement in the change. Meeting students' needs is an important factor that could encourage teachers to try different ways to reach their students. Students and teachers need to build positive relationships; students who can demonstrate their comprehension are more inclined to respect and relate to the teachers who help them achieve their levels of competency. Many teachers looked at change more positively when they saw their students reacting positively to more student-directed activities. When teachers had the time to interact with students individually due to the longer class periods, the teachers felt stronger connections with their students and made even a stronger effort to make this change work.

Teachers' Involvement in Training

Shadle Park High School teachers were committed to providing training that met their needs as teachers, and they sought out consultants that met their criteria and developed a training schedule that worked efficiently for them. Having training bolstered their courage. Their training throughout the summer made a major difference for teachers who planned all summer and were ready to begin their school year. Teachers knew, when those plans were at an end, that they needed more training in order to be successful in the block schedule.

Kettle Falls teachers did not have as much training as Shadle Park High School. As a smaller staff, however, they spent a great deal of time assisting one another. They also made suggestions for training, which they researched, and they visited other schools going through this process, met with teachers in their departments, and learned from them successful teaching strategies. Once the change was implemented, the emotions changed to fear, anger, and excitement for some teachers—and for other teachers, joy.

Administrators' Role in Facilitating This Change

Administrators can be the building force for the success, or failure, of the move to the block schedule. By providing teachers with a meaningful role in the planning and developing of the schedule, the training, and the implementation of the change process, administrators demonstrate their confidence and professional trust in the teachers. The actions of principals affect the staff, students, and community. Administrators who keep in mind that change is a personal issue with each teacher and that individuals respond uniquely to change will find themselves more able to understand the process each teacher is experiencing. Hargreaves (1994) warned against administrators overriding teachers' own desires for change. Hargreaves indicated that the people within the school create whatever change that occurs and lasts.

This kind of systemic change that puts administrators in a supportive role and teachers in a decision-making role may require more effort from administrators than a directive role would require. Leadership may come through both teachers and administrators. The principal needs to protect the autonomy of all of the teachers by guarding against a few teachers attempting to control the decision-making process. Administrators become facilitators who work to ensure that teachers are involved in both faculty decisions and in their own training and development. Administrators not only provide the avenue for teachers to take major responsibilities for the change process but also administrators are responsible for keeping all teachers involved, giving them support, and evaluating their progress.

It is human nature to put one's personal interest first. An administrator helps keep those teachers who are struggling actively involved to keep them from feeling isolated through their own fears. Teachers who become angry, depressed, or uncooperative are not showing bad morale—they are grieving for the loss of what they have always done—and felt successful doing.

Administrators have another important role: protecting the students and teachers from interruptions and frequent adjustments that cause disruptions in the schedule. Evaluating the time out of classes for assemblies with the least effect on the overall program was a major challenge. At Kettle Falls, I fell short in seeing all of the areas the change in time could affect. I had to make adjustments, and I needed input from teachers to make the adjustments effective and workable. Working with the teachers with even minor changes saved me several errors and many hard feelings from staff members.

Administrators need to attend to the evaluation process for teachers earlier in the school year, give assistance as needed to either bring the teacher up to the standard that the block requires or provide the teacher with a different career direction than this school. Administrators want teachers to take risks and to change as needed to accommodate the longer time frame. The balance between risk-taking and hurting students is difficult for an administrator to measure, but the administrator completes the evaluation form for each teacher, and this form needs to reflect the teacher's performance accurately. The administrator has the responsibility to encourage teachers to take risks as they adjust to the new time frame. At the same time, the administrator is responsible for the quality of the education of students in every classroom.

As principal, I found that balance of encouraging risk-taking and providing quality education for students both interesting and challenging. Some professional educators need the security of permission to risk throughout the change process. Other teachers enjoy the risk and jump into the unknown with enthusiasm. I have been personally and professionally enriched by the gambit of challenges teachers have been willing to accept and I have felt renewed professionally as I have worked with teachers seeking new directions in their delivery of information. I have also felt professionally challenged by the few teachers who seemed locked into years of teaching methods that are not working in the block schedule. At times, I sought outside assistance. Failure could cause a teacher to give up his or her career. I brought in professional help to assist teachers who were unable to move on their own to more effective ways to teach in this schedule, and the teachers and I were grateful for that choice.

I used the evaluation tool to encourage change, not as a negative scare tactic, and I made adjustments that reflected the improvements as teachers' performances showed progress. I felt the need to lift and support teachers as they developed positively in this change process, and I did not make any other major changes during this school year.

Amy noted that Shadle Park High School teachers became tired and stressed. Amy advised that the school needs to focus on just the block schedule and find time for teachers to work with one another and support one another in new classes. Amy stated, "Let's protect and support the teachers throughout the year of change. We need to respect them in these challenging times."

Summary

This chapter has developed each section of the previous chapters. In addition to these topics, I have explained themes involving emotional and physical changes which teachers experience while entering the change process and while the change process was taking place. I have shared teachers' involvement in physical changes, including planning, training, student management, and other related topics. I have also indicated teachers' emotional changes, including pride, grief, a sense of accomplishment and failure, fear, and other emotional responses to change.

Teacher involvement in researching, planning, and implementing the block schedule was important to both administrators and teachers at both Shadle Park High School and Kettle Falls High School. Teachers experienced professional and personal confusion and frustration to varying degrees, depending upon their individual abilities to adjust to change. The challenge seemed almost overwhelming in some cases, but the reactions of some teachers were professionally and personally uplifting and reaffirmed their teaching abilities and their abilities to grow professionally.

Training seemed to help most teachers, but actually experiencing the block schedule on a daily basis brought out the need for more time for collaboration among colleagues, more individual time for planning, and more training. Relationships between teachers and students changed with the longer contact time per period. Teachers indicated positive change with better relationships with students. When a student and teacher had a conflict, the longer period was not always the solution to or the cause of the problem. Many teachers indicated a desire for more training once they were actually involved with students in the block schedule.

Administrators facilitated the change process in many ways. Securing funding for training and teacher time, providing teachers with decision-making power to plan the change process, and planning departmentally and individually were three ways administrators supported staff. Using the evaluation process to guide, assist, and allow risk-taking—and not as a negative tool helped as well. The physical changes and the emotional responses of the teachers and administrators in this study were intertwined, and dependent upon one another as the change process unfolded.

CHAPTER VI: CONCLUSION

Shadle Park High School moved from a seven-period day to an AB block schedule for the 1996-1997 school year after considering and planning previous years. This study explored this process of change from a traditional schedule to a block schedule at this school. My professional and personal involvement with a similar change when I was an administrator at Kettle Falls High School prompted me to become involved in this qualitative study incorporating elements of heuristic inquiry. Heuristic inquiry evolves through a researcher who has had similar changes, and the researcher and the subjects of the study examine together the nature of the experience. Having participated in a similar change, I hope my insights into the experience have brought depth to the research without biasing results.

A review of the literature related to organizations and how change affects the people and the organizations where change occurred. Emotional changes, the importance of building trust among participants, and the overall goal of creating change to improve the educational experience featured administrators, teachers, students, and parents experiencing the change process with many emotional reactions throughout the change process. Specifically, I have provided the reader the opportunity to experience the change process as related by ten teachers and two administrators.

The benefits of block scheduling have made it a worthwhile endeavor, even though the process of change is difficult to varying degrees for all participants. When high school teachers can meet with approximately half of their students daily, instead of all of them, teachers have more opportunities to get to know their students' learning styles, which helps them design lessons that accommodate students' various learning styles. When students have fewer classes to deal with, prepare for, pay attention to, and attend each day, they have an increased opportunity to learn more. Meeting four teachers' expectations rather than seven or eight teachers per day is a major stress reliever for most students. Just eliminating the passing time between classes from six times to two or three times cuts behavior problems and disciplinary action by much more than half.

Both Shadle Park High School and Kettle Falls High School still use a form of unique scheduling. I have to conclude that it is working for them and their communities. I am grateful that I had this opportunity to be involved with both schools and the research project. Change isn't easy, for sure. But change for the better, as these schools have shown, has had long-term benefits for many students, teachers, and administrators. Change of this magnitude is more easily attained when all participants are part of the decision-making process and not "surprised" with this major change in teaching and learning for everyone involved.

The research sources used for this dissertation hold as true today as many of them did several years ago. The change process is not easy, for sure, and the educators who provided incites into this process have had, and still have, a powerful message to share with any school organization considering using time differently to improve their educational system. Research continues in this general area because many more schools are searching for ways to better serve their students and their communities. I encourage every educator to become informed by conducting personal and professional research on how systemic change may give students and teachers a safer, more effective learning experience. I especially recommend that teachers and administrators concentrate on the importance of teaching every student every day. Educators need to continue to be aware of the uniqueness of each student's life experiences and how the growing and development process happens uniquely to them. We teach students first. We guide them toward having success in their future. To do this, we can follow Mr. Rogers' three rules for success: "1. Be Kind. 2. Be Kind. 3. Be Kind."

APPENDIX

Behavior Consequences Regarding Suspensions/Expulsions

Behavior Consequences Involving Suspensions And Expulsions Need to be Modified or Dropped in Public Schools Substitutions for the usual "detention" School Community Service. We cannot teach students who are not in school. To stop punitive detentions, our school used the assigning of Community Service Choices. Any student could do community service, and awards were given at the end of the school year.

Students may choose from a list of opportunities to provide a service to others during lunchtime at school, after school, at home, or in the community. Possibilities for their choosing include, and are definitely not limited to, the following:

**Having lunch with a new student and giving him/her a tour of the school.

**Assisting teachers with NON PUNITIVE JOBS that teachers come up with, based on knowledge of what an individual student or groups of students like to do. For examples:

**The Home Ec teacher needs help baking and/or decorating desserts or assembling printed work for classes.

**A Shop teacher may have an engine he knows kids like to take apart/put together/make work. He assigns help with this engine to "prepare for class".

**Students may tutor other students under the teacher's direction.

**Students may choose to do community service during lunchtime or after school. This may help parents with transportation concerns, especially for students who ride the bus home. Choosing lunchtime can eliminate the need for parents to leave work early or arrange transportation to provide students with rides home.

Teachers are encouraged to develop a list of items students may do based on the classes they teach that are not viewed by students as punishment.

Community representatives may have pre-approved jobs students may want to do, such as snow shoveling at a convalescent home/hospital/etc.

Specific arrangements for community service duties with local churches may serve as excellent opportunities for students to assist in ways that fit public school requirements.

In-school Suspension (but not isolation)

Teachers will provide work students have missed and will miss while they are on in-school suspension. The essential goal for each student is that each student is fully prepared for work in the classes they are missing, so when they return to school the next school day, they are fully prepared to participate in their classes.

During the "suspension":

Each teacher will visit the student twice during the day to be sure he/she understands the work assigned and that the student is doing it correctly.

During these visits, teachers will attempt to establish a positive connection with the students, talk pleasantly and kindly, assist politely—set a good example. Our hope is that the student will come back feeling welcome in each class, not feel that the teacher does not like him/her or want him/her back in class. Since the work for the next day is done, the student will not be lost or behind, or unable to participate.

The school counselor will meet with the student twice during the day to help the student feel supported and see how things are at home and school for this student.

The principal will meet with the student and be sure each student has a good lunch, restroom breaks, and a chance to also establish a positive rapport.

Substitute for Expulsion

Students who reach a point where they cannot successfully attend classes may need another way to succeed.

Part-time schedule in-school and part-time online under the school's direction.

Full-time online under the school's direction. This may be done on campus.

Quarter classes, rather than semester classes.

Part-time school schedule as supervised by school personnel and part-time work schedule through the school or through parent supervision.

Course packets issued to students weekly and graded for credit. The student may work his/her way back into school and earn credit—or take an approved brief break from attending classes with parental supervision if desired.

Teachers, Counselors, School Staff, Parents, and Students will be encouraged to participate in developing humane alternatives for the traditional punishments presently or previously required as a result of a broken rule at school. Together we can provide humane education that benefits all key participants, including the community and especially the students.

whwhwhwhwhwhwhwhwhwhwhwhwhwhwhwhwhwhwhwhwhwhwhwhwhwhwhwh

What Happened?

Sarah and her 40th Reunion

When the email came telling Sarah about her 40th reunion from high school, she read through the plans: Saturday lunch at the high school cafeteria, a tour of the remodeled high school, and an evening of dinner and socializing at a local restaurant-bar with a Sunday afternoon gathering at the city park. Sarah thought about the old school and was glad that it had been remodeled. She thought about the lunch, dinner, and Sunday gathering. Then she let herself think about who would be attending and who she might sit with or enjoy visiting with at these events.

Background: Sarah did not have a positive experience during her high school years. She was a country girl, had lots of animals to feed, a large garden to help grow and harvest, and many household chores to do because her mother was often not well, and her father had a business that kept him away from home often. She and her sisters were frequently absent from school to help at home. She had few social opportunities, and when she thought about whom she would visit at the reunion, she couldn't think of even one friend. Not one person, she thought, would remember her as a friend, let alone want to spend time with her. Sarah felt that any visit she participated in with former classmates would take time away from their visiting others who truly were their friends.

What could have happened? Sarah could have had a better high school experience if the school had provided opportunities for their students to learn how to interact socially, learn how to contribute to class as active learners, and have teachers who made a point to know all of their students, reach out to them, show respect for them, and create an environment that was friendly, open, safe, and caring. With support, Sarah could have remembered high school with at least some positive memories. She also could attend this reunion and find it enjoyable—or not very enjoyable.

What did happen? Sarah graduated from high school, and she decided to attend college. By working several jobs and taking out government loans, she graduated and earned her teaching certificate. She started out teaching like she was taught—teacher-centered lessons. She became friends with another teacher who had a student-centered approach. After seeing her friend in action and watching her students involved in their learning, Sarah gradually gave up her "sage on stage" approach and used group learning and a student-centered approach.

Sarah chose not to attend her high school reunion. Based on the emails classmates were sending among themselves, Sarah was not included in any of the individual and small group messages encouraging classmates to attend. For Sarah, facing another possibility of being left out of interactions, ignored, or simply unrecognized was not something she did not need to experience again as an adult. She had a good life, she has family and friends in her current life, and she saw no reason to put herself in a negative position. Returning to her hometown was a very long drive to take a chance. "Once I graduated from high school, my life just got better and better," Sarah commented. I wish high school had been better, but looking back at the bullying I endured and the isolation I felt, I am happy to enjoy my present life and leave the past behind.

How does this relate to our topic? When we involve our students in classes, using a variety of learning methods—project learning, team projects, and opportunities for students to interact appropriately with one another and with teachers, we give them a special gift: being able to socially interact in positive ways. Sarah's classmates lost out by not getting to know Sarah—or her getting to know them. Sarah, fortunately, survived on her own. Teachers can include students in active group learning in their classes, especially students who are not sure how to participate. Successful social interaction is a life skill that fits well into school learning and that will serve students throughout their lives as participating citizens.

whwhwhwhwhwhwhwhwhwhwhwhwhwhwhwhwhwhwhwhwhwhwhwhwhwhwhwh

The Spokesman Review Guest Editorial

Behavior Can Be Improved Humanely in Schools

by Marie Phillips, Ph.D

While schools are planning to provide a healthy school experience, in-school or online, full-time or part-time, I encourage everyone to take a strong look at the long-practiced system of assigning punishment for various infractions—all listed in The Student Handbook for any school (usually online). I have been both teacher and administrator in Washington State schools and three other states, and looking back over my years as an educator. I see clearly now what I deeply wish I would have seen throughout my career. Too often, we lose students from school by trying to punish them into cooperating instead of guiding them toward success. This is a national issue, not just Washington State.

Most student handbooks list consequences when a student is tardy. Punishments include detentions and suspensions from school. Another disciplinary section involves unexcused absences—with consequences that include in-school and out-of-school suspensions, being unable to make up work,—and expulsion. A student coming back to school following a suspension will be behind academically in every class. These students are often left to survive on their own. If they cannot catch up successfully, they fail classes.

We need a behavior system based on keeping students in school, not having them work their way toward expulsion, and facing the difficulties that may follow—which could affect the rest of their lives in negative ways.

More boys than girls receive major consequences. According to www.discriminology.org, 70% of law enforcement referrals from schools are minority students: Black, Latino, American Indian, and 68% of male prisoners in federal prison do not have a high school diploma. Homelessness, unemployment, drug abuse, mental illness, crime, and prison are stronger possibilities for non-graduates. Once students get known for missing school or settling for failure, they may not see a way through their situation. And worse for these students, discrimination rears up to crush them as well.

We CAN figure this out. As a high school principal, I assigned a student to "On Task" for truancy. Teachers provided the work the student missed, along with at least two visits to the student during the day to encourage the student and make sure the student knew how to do the work. The counselor met at least twice with the student for support. I also met with him/her for further support. When the student came to school the next day, classwork was done, and the staff was supportive. For most students, one day like this was a major cure for truancy. The usual punishment system is failing too many. Counselors, administrators, teachers, and staff need to focus their attention on students' well-being and look for ways to lift students, not seek for rule infractions to punish them.

Sometimes students face horrendous issues at home that cause them to be late or absent. Students come to school with all their issues—we need to keep them attending and successful, not shut them out. Some students take a stand to reject help. Some students are amazingly hard to work with or have undiagnosed disabilities, but we cannot give up on them. Every student shapes our nation's future. School personnel must meet students where they are and guide them toward making choices that enrich their future.

The Community High School in Spokane has a principal and staff who focus on students succeeding. Serious disciplinary issues usually begin with a parent-student-principal conference to find a new path to success. When students have conflicts with one another, the principal brings them together to find ways students can resolve issues between them instead of letting anger bring future unrest. If this school can take the fear of punishment out of school, other schools with a punishment focus can redirect, and do this, too. I know that there are many schools that are meeting this challenge with success. There are too many schools that are stuck in the past and keep doing what has always been done: make a mistake, get punished. Students deserve better.

Covid-19 has become a major issue in schools. Bringing behavior upgrades along with this healthy change will also provide a healthier, happier environment.

BIBLIOGRAPHY

Adams, D., & Salvaterra, M. (1997). Block Scheduling: Pathway to Success. Lancaster, PA: Technomic Publishing Co.

America 2000, An Educational Strategy: (1991), Washington, DC: U. S. Printing Office.

Anderson, D. (1996, January), Four Period Day Network News, Wenatchee, WA: North Central ESD.

Anderson, L. (1993), "What Time Tells Us," Timepiece: Extending and Enhancing Learning Time, Reston, VA., National Association of Secondary School Principals.

Angus, Ll. (1989), "New Leadership and the Possibility of Educational Reform," In J. Smith (Ed), Critical Perspectives on Educational Leadership, (pp. 63-92), New York, NY: The Falmer Press.

Annie E. Casey Foundation (2021), https.datacenter.kidscount.org., Statistics on discrimination in public schools in America.

Babbie, E. (1995), The Practice of Social Research, Belmont, CA: Wadsworth Publishing Company.

Ballinger, C. (1993), "Year-round Education: It's Time," Timepiece: Extending and Enhancing Learning time, Reston, VA: NASSP.

Banathy, B. H. (1991). Systems Design of Education: A Journey to Create the Future, Englewood Cliffs, NJ: Educational Technology Publications.

Bass, B. (1990), Bass & Stogdill's Handbook of Leadership: Theory, Research & Managerial Applications, New York, NY: The Free Press.

Berman, P. & McLaughlin, M. W. (1977), Federal Programs Supporting Educational Change: Vol. VII Factors Affecting Implementation and Continuation, Santa Monica, CA: Rand Corporation.

Berry, B. (1995). School Reform in Chattanooga: An Independent Report on Chattanooga Public Schools Middle Grades Reform Initiatives, 1994-1995, Southern Education Foundation, Atlanta, GA.

Blank, W. & Scaglione, J. (1992), Integrating Academic and Vocational Education: Second in a Series, Tallahassee, FL: Florida Department of Education.

Block, P. (1987). The Empowered Manager: Positive Political Skills at Work, San Francisco, CA: Jossey-Bass Publishers.

Bolman, L. G, & Deal, L. G. (1984), Modern Approaches to Understanding and Managing Organizations, San Francisco, CA: Jossey-Bass Publishers.

Bottoms, G. & Presson, A. (1991), Reaching the Goal to Reduce the Drop-out Rate, Atlanta, GA: Southern Regional Education Board.

Bradford, J. C., Jr. (1996, April), Year-round Schools: A Twenty-year Follow-up Study of a Nationally Recognized Single Track Four-quarter Plan at the High School Level, [Revised]. Paper presented at the annual meeting of the American Educational Research Association, New York, NY. (ERIC Document Reproduction Service No. ED 396 405).

Brewer, M., & Collins, B. (Eds.) (1981), Scientific Inquiry and the Social Sciences, San Francisco, CA: Jossey-Bass Publishers.

Bridges, W. (1980), Transitions: Making Sense of Life's Changes, New York, NY: Addison-Wesley Publishing Company.

Bridges, W. (1991), Managing Transitions: Making the Most of Change: Addison-Wesley Publishing Company.

Bruckner, M. (1997, December), "Eavesdropping on Change: Listening to Teachers during the First Year of an Extended Block Schedule," NASSP Bulletin, 81, 42-52.

Canady, R. L.. & Rettig, M. D. (1993), "Unlocking the Lockstep High School Schedule," Phi Delta Kappan, 75, 310-314.

Canady, R. L. & Rettig, M. D., (1995), Block Scheduling: A Catalyst for Change in High Schools. Princeton, NJ: Eye on Education. (ERIC Document Reproduction Service No. Ed 387 930)

Carroll, J. M. (1989), The Copernican Plan: Restructuring the American High School, Andover, MA: Regional Laboratory for Educational Improvement of the Northeast and Islands.

Chen, David F., et al. (2020. "Effect of Block Scheduling on African American Male's High School Test Performance," JAEPR, 5 (1). University of North Carolina, Greensboro, NC.

Cherniss, C. (1995), Beyond Burnout: Helping Teachers, Nurses, Therapists, and Lawyers Recover from Stress and Disillusionment, New York, NY, Routledge Company.

Claxton, D. B. & Bryant, G. Jr. (1996, March), "Block Scheduling: What Does It Mean for Physical Education?" Journal of Physical Education, Recreation and Dance, 67, 48-50.

Clinton, W. (1997), "State of the Union Address," Washington, DC: U. S. Government Printing Office.

Commission on Excellence in Education (1983), A Nation at Risk, Washington, DC: U. S. Printing Office.

Commission on Student Learning (1996), Education Reform in Washington State, Olympia, WA: Office of the Superintendent of Public Instruction.

Conner, D. (1993), Managing at the Speed of Change, New York, NY: Villard Books.

Cook, T. & Reichardt, C. (1979), Qualitative and Quantitative Methods in Evaluation Research, Beverly Hills, CA: Sage Publications.

Craig, P. (1978), The Heart of a Teacher: A Heuristic Study of the Inner World of Teaching, Ann Arbor, MI: University Microfilm International.

Cresswell, R. A. & Rasmussen, P. (1996, December), "Developing a Structure for Personalizing in the High School," NASSP Bulletin, 81, 27-30.

Darling-Hammond, L. (1995), "Policy for Restructuring," In A. Lieberman, Ed., The Work of Restructuring Schools, New York, NY: Teachers College Press.

Davis-Wiley, P. and George, M. & Cozart, A. (1995, March), Block Scheduling in the Secondary Arena. Perceptions from the Inside, Paper presented at the annual meeting of the Midsouth Educational Research Association, Biloxi, MS. (ERIC Document Reproduction No. ED 393 177)

Day, M., Ivanov, C., & Binkley, S. (1996, September), "Tackling Block Scheduling: How to Make the Most of Longer Classes," Science Teacher, 63, 25-27.

Denzin, N. K. (1970) The Research Act in Sociology. London, EN: Butterworths.

Denzin, N. K. (1989) Interpretive Interactionism, Newberry Park, CA: Sage Publications.

Derrington, M. L. (1988), The Role of the Principal: Tradition, Transition and Transformation: An Ethnographic Study of Two High School Principals. Unpublished doctoral dissertation, University of Washington, Seattle.

Discriminology Beta (2021) www.discriminology.com, School Discrimination.

Dooley, P. J. (1992), In Pursuit of Change, Vancouver, BS: EduServ Inc.

Douglas, B. & Moustakas, C. (1984), Heuristic Inquiry: The Internal Search to Know, Detroit, MI: Center for Humanistic Studies.

Doyle, R. & Doyle, P. (1992), Gain Management, New York, NY: American Management Association.

English, F. W. (1993, "Changing the Cosmology of the School Schedule." Timepiece: Extending and Enhancing Learning time, Reston, VA: National Association of Secondary School Principals.

Fernandez, J. A.; with Underwood, J. (1993), Tales Out of School. New York, NY: Little, Brown and Company.

Fine, M. (1994), (1994), Chartering Urban School Reform: Reflections of Public High Schools in the Midst of Change, New York, NY: Teachers College Press.

Firestone, W. & Rosenblum, S. (1988), "Building Commitment in Urban High Schools," Education, Evaluation, and Policy Analysis, 10, 285-299.

Fitzgerald, R. (1996, September), "Brain-compatible Teaching in a Block Schedule, School Administrator, 53, 20-21, 24.

Fletcher, R. K. Jr. (1997), "A Study of the Block Scheduling Movement in Six High Schools in the Upper Cumberland Region of Tennessee," Revision of a paper presented at the annual meeting of the Tennessee Academy of Science, Sewanee, TN, November 1996. (ERIC Document Reproduction Service No. ED403 647)

Ford, P. J. (1995), "Some Thoughts on Resistance to Change," Unpublished manuscripts, Gonzaga University, Spokane, WA.

Ford, P. J. (1996), "Covenantal Leadership for the Third Millennium," Unpublished manuscript, Gonzaga University, Spokane, WA.

Fullan, M. G. (1993), Change Forces: Probing the Depths of Educational Reform, New York, NY: The Falmer Press.

Fullan, M. G. with Stiegelbauer, S. (1991), The Meaning of Educational Change, New York, NY: Teachers College Press.

Fullan, M. & Miles, M. (1992), "Getting Reform Right: What Works and What Doesn't," Kappan, 73, 744-752.

Gardner, J. W. (1990), On Leadership, New York, NY: The Free Press.

Gartner, R. E. & Sterzing, P. R. (2018). Social Ecological Correlates of Family-level Interpersonal and Environmental Micro Aggressions toward Sexual and Gender Minority Adolescents. Journal of Family Violence, 33(1), 1-16. https://doi.org/10.1007/s10896-o17-9937-0.

Gee, W. (1997, June), "The Copernican Plan and Year-round Education," Phi Delta Kappan, 78, 793-796.

Geismar, T. J. & Pullease, B. G. (1006, September), "The Trimester: A Competency-based Model of Block Scheduling," NASSP Bulletin, 80, 95-105.

Gerking, J. I. (1995, March), "Building Block Schedules," Science Teacher, 67, 28-30.

Gheraldi, S. & Turner, B. (19878), "Real Men Don't Collect Soft Data," Quaderno 13, Departimento di Policia Sociale, Universita di Trento.

Glaser, B. & Strauss, A. (1967), The Discovery of Grounded Theory, Chicago, IL: Aldine.
Glasser, W. (1990), The Quality School, New York, NY: Harper and Row.

Glickman, C. D. (1990), Renewing America's Schools: A Guide for School-based Action, San Francisco, CA: Jossey-Bass Publishers.

Gonzales, S. A. (1994), An Observable Case Study of Issues Related to Site-based Shared Decision Making, Unpublished doctoral dissertation, Harvard University, Cambridge, MS.

Goldbach, J. T., Sterzing, P. R., & Stuart, M. J. (2018). "Challenging Conventions of Bullying Thresholds: Exploring Differences Between Low and High Levels of Bully-only, Victim-only, and Bully-victim Roles. Journal of Youth and Adolescence, 47(3), 586-600. https://doi.org/10.1007/s10964-017-0775-4.

Goodlad, J. I. (1984), A Place Called School, New York, NY: McGraw-Hill.

Greenleaf, R. K. (1977), Servant Leadership, New York, NY: Paulist Press.

Guilfoyle, K. (1994), Restructuring the American High School: A Case Study in California, Unpublished doctoral dissertation, University of Southern California, Los Angeles.

Guskey, T. R. & Kifer, E. (1995, April), Evaluation of a High School Block Schedule Restructuring Program, Paper presented at the annual meeting of the American Educational Research Association, San Francisco, CA. (ERIC Document Reproduction Service No. ED 384 652).

Hackman, D. (1995, September), "Improving School Climate: Alternating-day Block Schedule," Schools in the Middle, 5, 28-33.

Hackman, D. (1996, November), "Ten Guidelines for Implementing Block Scheduling," Educational Leadership, 53, 24-27.

Hall, G. E. & Hord, S. M. (1987), Change in Schools: Facilitating the Process, Albany, NY: State University of New York Press.

Hansen, J. & Liftin, E. (1991), School Restructuring: A Practitioner's Guide, Swampscott, MA: Waterson Publishing Company.

Hargreaves, A. (1994), Changing Teachers, Changing Times, London, EN: Cassell.

Hord. S. (1987), Evaluating Educational Innovation, New York, NY: Croom Helm.

Hord S.; Rutherford, W.; Huling-Austin, L.; & Hall, G. (1987), Taking Charge of Change, Alexandria, VA: Association for Supervision and Curriculum Development.

Hoyt, R. I. (1996), The Institutionalization of Change in a Restructured High School: A Case Study, Unpublished doctoral dissertation, University of Nevada, Los Angeles, CA.

www.Huffpost.com (5/13/2014) Race, Disability and the School-To-Prison Pipeline.

Hurley, J. C. (1997a, December), "The 4x4 Block Scheduling Model: What Do Students Have to Say about It?" NASSP Bulletin, 81, 64-72.

Hurley, J. C. (1997b, December), "The 4x4 Block Scheduling Model: What Do Teachers Have to Say about It?" NASSP Bulletin, 81, 53-63.

Husserl, E. (1962), Ideas, New York, NY: Colliers Publishing.

Irmsher, K. (1996a, March), "Block Scheduling." ERIC Digest, No. 104, 2-3 (ERIC Document Reproduction Service No. ED 393 156)

Irmsher, K. (1996b, July) "Block Scheduling in High Schools." OSSC Bulletin, 39, 2-57. (ERIC Document Reproduction Service No. ED 399 673)

Isaacson, N. (1996), "The Human Costs of Reform, Organizational Caring, and the Douglas Fir." Unpublished manuscript, Gonzaga University.

Johnson, S. M. (1990), Teachers at Work: Achieving Success in Our Schools, New York, NY: Basic Books.

Kadel, S. (1994), Reengineering High Schools for Student Success: Hot Topics: Usable Research, Washington, DC: Office of Educational Research and Improvement.

Kane, C. (1994, September), Prisoners of Time Research, National Education Commission on Time and Learning, Washington, DC: Government Printing Office.

Klecher, B. & Lodman, W. (1996), "A Study of Principals' Openness to Change in 168 Restructuring Schools." Paper presented at the annual meeting of the American Educational Research Association, New York, NY: April 8-12, 1996.

Kruse, G. & Zulkoski, M. (1997), "The Northwest Experience: a Lesser Road Traveled," NASSP Bulletin, 81, 16-22.

Lewis, A. (1989), Restructuring America's Schools, Arlington, VA: American Association of School Administrators.

Lieberman, A. (Ed.) (1986), Rethinking School Improvement, New York: Teachers College Press.

Lieberman, A. (1995), The Work of Restructuring Schools, New York, NY: Teachers College Press.

Lieberman, A.; Darling-Hammond, L.; & Zuckerman, D. (1991, Early Lessons in Restructuring Schools, New York, NY: National Center for Restructuring Education, Schools and Teaching.

Lieberman, A. & Miller, L. (1990), "Restructuring Schools: What Matters and What Works," Kappan 7, 759-764.

Lincoln, Y. S. & Guba, E. G. (1985), Naturalist Inquiry, Beverly Hills, CA: Sage Publications, Inc.

Majchrzak, A. (1984), Methods for Policy Research, Newbury Park, CA: Sage Publications, Inc.

Marris, P. (1974), Loss and Change, New York, NY: Pantheon Books.

Merriam, S. B. (1988) Case Study Research in Education: A Qualitative Approach, San Francisco, CA: Jossey-Bass Publishers.

Miles, M. & Huberman, M. (1994), Qualitative Data Analysis, Thousand Oaks, CA: Sage Publications, Inc.

Mistretta, G. M. & Polansky, H. B. (1997, December), "Prisoners of Time: Implementing a Block Schedule in the High School," NASSP Bulletin 81, 23-31.

Moustakas, C. (1994), Phenomenological Research Methods, Thousand Oaks, CA: Sage Publications, Inc.

Munroe, M. J. (1989, February), Block: Successful Alternative Format Addressing Learner Needs. Paper presented at the annual conference of the Association of Teacher Educators, St. Louis, MI, (ERIC Document Reproduction Service No. ED 311-003)

Murphy, J. (1991), Reconstructing Schools: Capturing and Assessing the Phenomena, New York, NY: Teachers College Press.

National Association of Secondary School Principals (1996), Breaking Ranks: Changing an American Institution, San Francisco, CA Carnegie Foundation for the Advancement of Teaching.

National Science Teachers Association (1977), Block Scheduling: Teaching Strategies for the Restructured School Day, Arlington, VA: NSTA.

Neimeyer, R. (1992), The Block Schedule, Omak, WA: Omak High School Publication.

Newmann, F. M. (1993), "Beyond Common Sense in Educational Restructuring: The Issues of Content and Linkage," Educational Researcher, 22, 4-13.

North Carolina State Department of Public Instruction (1996), Foreign Language on the Block, Raleigh, NC: North Carolina State Department of Public Education. (ERIC Document Reproduction Service No. ED 403 742).

Norum, K. & Lowry, M. (1995), "The Heart of Educational Restructuring: Dealing with Change." Paper presented at the annual meeting of the Association for Educational Communications and Technology, Anaheim, CA: February 8-12, 1995.

Norwicki, J. (1992), A School as a Crucible of Change: A Case Study of Restructuring and a Faculty's Culture, Unpublished doctoral dissertation, University of Massachusetts at Boston, MS.

Patterson, J. (1997) Coming Clean about Organizational Change: Leadership in the Real World, Arlington, VA: American Association of School Administrators.

Patterson, J.; Purkey, S.; & Parker, J. (1986), Productive School Systems for a Nonrational World, Alexandria, VA: Association for Supervision and Curriculum Development.

Patton, M. Q. (1982), Practical Evaluation, Newbury Park, CA: Sage Publications, Inc.

Patton, M. Q. (1986), Utilization Focused Evaluation, Beverly Hills, CA: Sage Publications, Inc.

Patton, M. Q. (1990), Qualitative Evaluation and Research Methods, Newbury Park, CA: Sage Publications, Inc.

Peskin, A. (1988), "In Search of Subjectivity—One's Own," Educational Researcher, 17, 17-21.

Phillips, I. D. (1997, September), "On the Block," Techniques: Making Education and Career Connections, 72, 32-35.

Pisapia, J. & Westfall, A. (1997a), Alternative High School Scheduling: Student Achievement and Behavior. Research Report. Richmond, VA. Metropolitan Educational Research Consortium. (ERIC Document Reproduction Service No. ED 411 337)

Pisapia, J. & Westfall, A. (1997b), Alternative High School Scheduling: A View from the Student's Desk: Research Report, Richmond, VA: Metropolitan Educational Research Consortium. (ERIC Document Reproduction Service No. ED 411 336)

Pisapia, J. & Westfall, A. (1997c) Alternative High School Scheduling: A View from the Teacher's Desk. Research Report. Richmond, VA: Metropolitan Research Consortium. (ERIC Document Reproduction No. ED 411 335)

Reid, L. (1995, March, Perceived Effects of Block Scheduling on the Teaching of English, Fort Collins, CO: Colorado State University (ERIC Document Reproduction Service No. ED 382 950)

Reid, W. (1995), Restructuring Secondary Schools with Extended Time Blocks and Intensive Courses: The Experiences of School Administrators in British Columbia. Unpublished doctoral dissertation, Gonzaga University, Spokane, WA.

Rettig, M. D. (2016, November), "The Effects of Block Scheduling." AASA the School Superintendents Association.

Rettig, M. D. & Canady, R. L. (1995, December), "When Can I Have Your Kids? Scheduling Specialist Teachers." Here's How, 14, 2-5.

Rettig, M. D. & Canady, R. L. (1996, September), "All Around the Block: The Benefits and Challenges of a Nontraditional School Schedule." School Administrator, 53, 8-14.

Reynolds, D. & Parker, A. (1992), Schools Effectiveness and School Improvement in the 1990's. London EN: Cassell.

Ruscoe, G. & Whitford, B. (1991, April), Qualitative and Quantitative Perspectives on Teacher Attitudes: The Third Year, Paper presented at the annual meeting of the American Educational Research Association, Chicago, IL. (ERIC Document Reproduction No. ED 336 351)

Sarason, S. (1983), Schooling in America, Scapegoat and Salvation, New York, NY: Free Press.

Sarason, S. (1990), The Predictable Failure of Education Reform, San Francisco, CA: Josey-Bass Publishers.

Schaef, A. & Fassel, D. (1988), The Addictive Organization, San Francisco, CA: Harper & Row.

Schon, D. (1971), Beyond the Stable State, New York, NY: Norton Publishing Company.

Senge, P. M. (1990), The Fifth Discipline, New York, NY: Doubleday Publishing Co.

Shils, E. (1959), "Social Inquiry and Autonomy of the Individual," In D. Lerner (Ed.), The Human Meaning of the Social Sciences, pp. 114-157, Cleveland, OH: Meridian Books, Inc.

Shockey, B. P. (1997), The Effects of Varying Retention Intervals within a Block Schedule on Knowledge Retention in Mathematics, Unpublished doctoral dissertation, University of Maryland, College Park. (ERIC Document Reproduction Service No. ED 415 093)

Shortt, T. L. & Thayer, Y. V. (1997, December), "A Vision for Block Scheduling: Where Are We Now? Where Are We Going?" NASSP Bulletin, 81, 1-15.

Singh, K. L. (1992), From Carnegie to Copernican: A Working Conference on Restructuring the High School. Tallahassee, FL: Florida State University.

Sizer, K. L. (1992), Horace's Compromise: The Dilemma of the American High School, Boston, MS: Houghton, Mifflin Co.

Sizer, T. R. (1992), Horace's School: Redesigning the American High School, New York, NY: Houghton Mifflin Co.

Slavin, R. (1990), Cooperative Learning: Theory, Research, and Practice. Englewood Cliffs, NJ: Prentice-Hall.

Snyder, D. (1997, October), 4-Block Scheduling: A Case Study of Data Analysis of One High School after Two Years, Paper presented at the annual meeting of the Midwest Educational Research Association, Chicago, IL. (ERIC Document Reproduction Service No. ED 414 626)

Spencer, W. A. & Lowe, C. (1994), The Use of Block Periods for Instruction: A Report and Evaluation. Paper presented at the annual conference: The Midsouth Educational Research Association, Nashville, TN. (ERIC Document Reproduction Service No. ED 378 941)

Stake, R. E. (1995), The Art of Case Study Research, Thousand Oaks, CA: Sage Publications, Inc.

Stemnock, S. K. (1975), The Four-day School Week, Arlington, VA: Educational Research Report (ERS).

Sterzing, P. R., Gibbs, J. J., Gartner, R. E. & Goldbach, J. T. (2018), "Bullying Victimization Trajectories for Sexual Minority Adolescents: Stable Victims, Resisters, and Late-onset Victims," 28(2), 368-378. https://doi.org/10.1111/jora. 12336.

Stuck, G. B. & Wyne, M. (1982, September), "Time and Learning: Implications for the Classroom Teacher. The Elementary School Journal, 83, 67-75.

Syropoulow, M. (1996, Summer), "A Supplemental Program for At-risk Ninth Graders: Evaluation of the Ninth Grade Project at Derby High School." ERS Spectrum, 14, 17-26.

Tadlock, M. & Barrett-Roberts, J. (1995), Middle Level Education in Small Rural Schools, Columbus, OH: National Middle School Association. (ERIC Document Reproduction Service No. ED 396 840)

Tesch, R. (1990), Qualitative Research, New York, NY: The Falmer Press.

Thomas, C. & Connell, R. (1997a, May), Parent Perceptions of Block Scheduling in a New York State High School. Paper presented at the annual meeting of the New England Educational Research Organization, Portsmouth, NH. (Eric Document Reproduction Service No. ED 409 644)

Thomas, C. & Connell, R. (1997b, October), Student Perceptions of Block Scheduling in a New York State High School. Paper presented at the annual meeting of the Northeastern Educational Research Association, Ellenville, NY. (ERIC Document Reproduction Service No. ED 417 186)

Thomas, G. I. (1973), Administrator's Guide to the Year-round School, West Nyack, NY: Parker Publishing Co. Inc.

Walter, Tim. (2016), "Are Block Schedules the Stress Buster Students Need?" NEA Today (03/04/2016).

Webb, R. B. (1994), Shared Decision Making and School Restructuring in Life Oak County, New York, NY: Teachers College, Columbia University, National Center for Restructuring Education, Schools and Teaching.

Wertz, R. (1987, Winter), "Meaning and Research of Methodology: Psychoanalysis as a Human Science." Methods, 1, 91-135.

West, M. (1996, March), Block Schedule: Breaking the Barriers. Paper presented at the annual meeting of the Association for Supervision and Curriculum Development." New Orleans, LA. (ERIC Document Reproduction Service No. ED 400 607)

Whitla, D. K.; Bempechat, J.; Perrone, V.; & Carroll, B. B. (1992, May). "The Masconomet Regional High School Renaissance Program: The First Implementation of the Copernican Plan." Cambridge, MS: Harvard Evaluation Team.

Wilson, C. (1995, May), "The 4:4 Block System: A Workable Alternative, NASSP Bulletin, 79, 63-65. (ERIC Document Reproduction Service No. ED 504 652)

Wisconsin Association of Foreign Language Teachers. (1995), Redesigning High School Schedules: A Report of the Task Force on Block Scheduling. Whitewater, WI: WAFLT. (ERIC Document Reproduction Service No. ED 382 950)

Wolfe, R. O. (1993), Synergy: Increasing Productivity with People, Ideas, and Things. Dubuque, IO: Kendall-Hunt Publishing Co.

Yukl, G. (1994), Leadership in Organizations, Englewood, NJ: Prentice-Hall, Inc.

Zahniser, Steven (2020). ""What is Agriculture's Share of the Overall US Economy?" USDA Economic Research Service, Washington, DC. https://ers.usda.gov.

Zaltman, G. & Duncan, R. (1977), Strategies for Planned Change, New York, NY: Wiley-Interscience Publication.

Zaragosa, N. (1997), Rethinking Language Arts: Passion and Practice: Vol. 9. Critical Education Practice Series. Hamden,CT: Garland Publishing, Inc.

Author's note: References include many from early research. Both past and present research blend well and have a great deal in common regarding schedule changes and enrichment opportunities for growth for both teachers and students in our nation's schools. I encourage readers to review these references, and investigate the multitude of current references available on both scheduling options and ways to make schools a better place for students to develop into positive citizens and for teachers to experience professional leadership roles. The use of creative scheduling is growing rapidly in secondary schools. Our students are our future. Well-prepared students become citizens who protect our democracy and our way of life. Creative scheduling and staff development can change their fears to success in teaching in positive ways.

ABOUT THE AUTHOR

Dr. Marie Phillips grew up in Montana and worked as a waitress, cook, baker, motel maid, farmer, hod carrier, and carpenter's apprentice during summers and after school. She attended Carroll College in Helena, Montana, and worked as an assistant secretary and music librarian. Her work, a small music scholarship, and government loans covered her education expenses. Her first teaching position was in Idaho.

Because she wanted to travel and see the world, she became a flight attendant for Pan American Airways. She was based first in New York, flying to Europe, Latin America and South America. She transferred to Seattle, Washington and flew to Alaska, Hawaii, Asia, The Philippines and New Zealand.

Teaching English, speech, drama, debate, and fine arts became the focus of her education career for many years in five states: Idaho, Montana, North Carolina, Florida, and Washington. Marie earned her Masters Degree in Educational Leadership and her secondary principal endorsement at the University of Montana, and she was a high school principal in Montana and Washington state. She earned her Ph.D. and her superintendent endorsement from Gonzaga University while employed as an adjunct professor. She served as Pre-K-12 superintendent in Washington state for nine years.

Dr. Phillips' goal in writing this book is to improve the educational process for both students and teachers. During her teaching and administration career, she has learned from students and colleagues that schools can provide education in a kind, compassionate way by making students and teachers the focus of education. Too often both students and teachers leave schools intentionally or through disciplinary actions rather than being encouraged to stay and be successful. She believes that schools can provide a humane educational experience, and she has devoted her later years to convincing others that improving schools will enrich our nation. Education humanely applied will reduce homelessness, unemployment, and the pipeline to prison. We need an attitude adjustment that makes students the main focus of education, taught by well-respected teachers. Students are our future, and teachers guide the way.

www.ingramcontent.com/pod-product-compliance
Lightning Source LLC
Chambersburg PA
CBHW071622030726
47598CB00001B/385